ASPATORE
Executive Business Intelligence

ASPATORE
Executive Business Intelligence

www.Aspatore.com

Aspatore is the most exclusive business book/brief/journal publisher in the world, publishing only the biggest names in the business world, including C-level leaders (CEO, CTO, CFO, COO, CMO, Partner) from over half the world's 500 largest companies and other leading executives. Aspatore publishes the Inside the Minds, Bigwig Briefs, Focusbook and Aspatore Business Review imprints in addition to other best selling business books, journals and briefs. By focusing on publishing only the biggest name executives, Aspatore provides readers with proven business intelligence from industry insiders, rather than relying on the knowledge of unknown authors and analysts. Aspatore focuses on publishing traditional print books and journals, while our portfolio company, Corporate Book Agents, focuses on developing areas within the book-publishing world. Aspatore is committed to providing our readers, authors, bookstores, distributors and customers with the highest quality books, book related services, and publishing execution available anywhere in the world.

The *Bigwig Briefs* Series
Condensed Business Intelligence From Industry Insiders
www.BigwigBriefs.com

Bigwig Briefs features condensed business intelligence from industry insiders and are the best way for business professionals to stay on top of the most pressing issues. *Bigwig Briefs* features knowledge excerpts from the best selling business books published by Aspatore books, other leading business book publishers, and essays written by leading executives for inclusion in a particular brief. *Bigwig Briefs* is revolutionizing the business book market by providing the highest quality content in the most condensed format possible for business book readers worldwide.

About Corporate Book Agents

Corporate Book Agents assists leading companies and select individuals with book writing, publisher negotiations, book publishing, book sponsorship, worldwide book promotion and generating a new revenue stream from publishing. Services also include white paper, briefing, research report, bulletin, newsletter and article writing, editing, marketing and distribution. The goal of Corporate Book Agents is to help our clients capture the attention of prospective customers, retain loyal clients and penetrate new target markets by sharing valuable information in publications and providing the highest quality content for readers worldwide. For more information please visit www.CorporateBookAgents.com or e-mail jonp@corporatebookagents.com.

BIGWIG BRIEFS:
THE ART OF DEAL MAKING

Leading Deal Makers Reveal the Secrets to Negotiating,
Leveraging Your Position and Inking Deals

ASPATORE
Executive Business Intelligence

Published by Aspatore Books, Inc.
For information on bulk orders, sponsorship opportunities or any other questions please email store@aspatore.com. For corrections, company/title updates, comments or any other inquiries please email info@aspatore.com.

First Printing, 2002
10 9 8 7 6 5 4 3 2 1

ISBN 1-58762-100-2

Library of Congress Card Number: 2001119818

Edited By Emily Dunn

Cover design by Rachel Kashon, Kara Yates, Ian Mazie

Special thanks also to: Ted Juliano, Tracy Carbone, and Rinad Beidas

BIGWIG BRIEFS:
THE ART OF DEAL MAKING

CONTENTS

BIGWIG BRIEFS:
THE ART OF DEAL MAKING

Joseph A. Hoffman, Arter & Hadden, Partner and Chairman of the Corporate/Securities Practice Group

Characteristics of a Great Deal Maker

A successful deal maker gets things done on time. Time kills deals. When situations linger, the parties involved may change their minds. A recent client we represented in an individual capacity was involved in a deal that was prolonged because the seller of the business wanted to postpone the deal for a few months to receive favorable tax treatments. Then the market crashed, and the deal never closed. The opportunity to sell at a good price was forfeited because of the one-month delay.

A successful deal maker gets things done, but sometimes the best deal is the one that does not get made. In the process of due diligence, sometimes unavoidable issues arise. In another earlier deal, the quality of the revenue of the acquisition target was not what we anticipated because of some questionable billing practices. We decided not to proceed with the transaction. Everyone was disappointed because no one likes a dead deal, but the CEO believed that the thorough due diligence and the decision not to proceed saved the company the $300 million purchase price.

A successful deal maker does not get lost in theoretical issues. The client needs protection, but the attorney must also be practical about possible consequences. A successful deal maker listens to his client and assumes his client's perspective.

Rules for Negotiating Deals

In negotiations, be honest, fair, and reasonable. Part of the negotiation process is building credibility. The real goal is to never take unfair advantage of anyone. It is a small world, and you can acquire a reputation for credibility in the community by being honest, up-front, fair, and reasonable. Do not insist on unreasonable points on either side of the table. Never try to "pull a fast one" by sneaking in changes. In one instance, a client insisted on an unimportant issue that would create work for the other side. This insistence harmed his credibility with the other side.

Avoid emotions. Using anger and intimidation to make a point does a disservice to all involved. The other party's willingness to cooperate and negotiate is often compromised.

Present the appearance of being in control and being flexible about whether or not to do the deal. To be most effective, be willing to walk away from the table.

Be the custodian and drafter of documents in order to structure the contractual relationship to the best advantage of your client. If the other side is the drafter and specifies issues, arguments, and positions from scratch, they might raise issues about which they would be concerned. However, when they have to read a document or agreement prepared by us, they sometimes do not see what is "not" contained in the document or agreement.

The location of the negotiations can make a difference. Always negotiate on home turf to be comfortable and in control. In a recent deal, the seller wanted to negotiate in New York, but our client said no. Throughout the deal, we either met on the phone or in my office, so the seller was more inconvenienced. During the final crunch toward closing, they were not getting as much sleep as we were. Still, we worked around the clock to close within five days. It is always better to claim the "home court" advantage.

Technology is a great tool. Often, when working on a transaction with another law firm, we search a variety of databases for the last five deals the other firm has completed. We see the documents they have written and the points negotiated. There is so much information available now that taking a little time to look can formulate a good picture of the law firm's past negotiations. So when the firm says, "We never do that," we can counter with, "Well, what about the so-and-so deal, where you did…?" Doing homework and using information is advantageous. Knowledge is power.

Be an expert of the law. The client may discover too late, after his deal is done, that there were taxes or additional obligations due and payable by him, obligations that his lawyer did not mention.

In transactions, make sound, well-grounded arguments. Know the points needed to win. Be confident, which comes with experience. Some attorneys may know the right answer, but if they are not confident and do not make the points as if they really believe them, the other side will not be convinced. Neither will their client. Adopt a reasonable approach, and avoid asking for points that are extraordinary or not customary. Negotiating for unreasonable points can cause a loss of credibility. Keep discussions on a friendly basis; do not allow discussions to get out of hand. Once a situation turns unfriendly or unprofessional, everything tends to go downhill.

Best Advice

"Time kills deals." That phrase has a wide and frequent application. There is often only a small window of time to complete a transaction before market conditions change. Because it is hard to foresee the changes in market conditions, the window of opportunity can open and close suddenly and without warning.

A few years ago, we took public a golf equipment manufacturer. It was the largest IPO in the history of the U.S. golf industry – a $110 million IPO. The company was performing well. Approximately a month after we completed the IPO, the golf equipment industry collapsed, unforeseen by anyone working on the transaction. Stock prices tanked, and everything went downhill from there. If the IPO had been delayed by only two months, it might never have been completed.

Another client of ours was working for a seller of a business who wanted to delay the closing of a deal into the following year for tax reasons. They wanted to move the closing from the end of November to the beginning of January – just over a month. Unfortunately, the deal never closed. Instead of getting $6 or $7 million out of the deal, they now have a company that is basically on life support because market conditions changed, and the buyer became nervous, delayed the transaction further, and finally withdrew. The deal was killed the following April – all because the seller wanted to delay it for tax purposes.

The advice I give most frequently is: Do whatever it takes, within the bounds of ethics and the law, to meet the commitment. Our firm is committed to providing quality legal work, which can include working extended hours. Clients expect requests to be completed on a timely basis. We strive to meet or exceed the expectations of our clients.

My advice to anyone who wants to learn how to make deals is to find a mentor and learn to work on teams for his or her clients. Dive in and take ownership of projects. Read! An excellent book called *Anatomy of a Merger,* by James C. Freund, walks the reader through an acquisition agreement step by step. Freund was a senior partner at a well-known firm in New York. Many people have read his book and learned from his experiences.

Teamwork for Successful Deals

People who work on our teams have to take ownership and responsibility. In law firms, attorneys are the primary contact with their clients. Most of the clients I deal with are both friends and long-time business associates. When I ask other attorneys to serve on a client team, I want them to take ownership of that client relationship and be as responsible for the same high-quality work for the client as they would for their own clients.

Having competent team members is critical. Clients pay a substantial amount of money for the legal services we provide. It has been our experience that when we render services in a timely and competent manner, the client rarely questions the fees. But if your whole team has done a great job except for maybe one person, the client tends to focus on that one person. Their overall impression will be, "Yes, everything went great, except for this one person..." Everyone has to do his or her work and do whatever it takes to get the deal done. Our secretaries and administrative assistants are a very important part of our service. During a recent deal, two secretaries rotated while working twenty-four hours a day over a four-day period, and the clients really appreciated it. In a service business, this level of service showed an unwavering commitment to the client.

Golden Rules for Making Deals

❏ Be honest, fair, and reasonable, earning credibility in the process.

❑ Draft the documents.

❑ Control the situation.

❑ When hiring counsel to assist with deals, hire experienced people. If the deal is not within the expertise of the firm or attorneys involved, the client's interest is not served.

❑ Look for leverage points and opportunities for trade-offs.

❑ Have a negotiating game plan to get where the client needs to be.

❑ Think creatively in trying to solve problems. The object is not to beat up the opposition or to make them look bad, but to achieve a win-win situation.

Mark J. Macenka, Testa, Hurwitz & Thibeault, Partner and Chair of the Business Practice Group

Scoping out the Deal

The first thing you need to do as a deal maker is understand what your or your client's goals are and what the participants want to get out of the particular deal at hand. Part of that is identifying, from among the owners and managers, who the decision makers are and who will call the shots and decide what the appetite is for compromise.

It's also important to get a full sense of the leverage you bring to the table.

You must go through the same exercise with the opposite side, figuring out their goals and their reasons for being at the table. Make sure you can identify who their decision makers are, whether it's the people at the table, people back at the office who can second-guess decisions that are made during the negotiations, or – worst of all – a committee, which can add a lot of time to the process. Understand as much as you can about the other side's appetite for compromise and what kind of leverage they bring to the table. It's important to understand who may hold more cards and who ultimately can exercise more leverage in the negotiations.

The way to prepare for a deal varies depending on the subject matter, but in general I read as much as possible about the other side and try to understand their level of development, whether they're a startup or a venture-backed operation or a large, publicly traded company. In many cases you can find a lot of the information on the web: cash position, who their investors are, who is on their board of directors, what deals they have done before. It is important to understand, for example, if it is a product deal, where they need some of your client's technology, how important that product or technology is to their development efforts and their build-or-buy decision, and whether there is a second source out there on the market. If it's in the merger and acquisition context, find out which party needs the deal more, what their needs are, and whether they are cash-constrained or cash-rich. At this point, the deal is about strategic issues, non-legal issues – finding out who your opponent is and what motivations could be driving them.

Success = Building Partnerships

Assuming both parties view this deal as the beginning of a relationship, it is important that both sides feel they were successful in building a relationship that can carry them forward in a mutually satisfactory and profitable way. You can't get overly ambitious and negotiate such a deal for your client that the other side wakes up a month or six months later and realizes they really got the short end of the stick. Part of successful deal making is helping your client see six, twelve, or twenty-four months down the road, so they can understand where they may be and what situations they may be facing. It's giving the kind of advice that enables your client to see around the corner. By allowing them to see farther down the road, you can often help them come up with a position that is more acceptable to both sides.

The art of deal making is a combination of preparation, understanding the facts and the issues, employing leverage and experience judiciously, and tempering advice with practical suggestions and business savvy to make sure you don't let legal points drive the deal. You have to make sure that ultimately the deal is workable and that it will give the client and the business partner the outcome that they want. You always have to focus on the ultimate goal of the client and what they're trying to get out of it, and always try to move the ball to that goal. That doesn't necessarily mean identifying the thirty-six key issues or the twelve key issues and knocking each of them off one by one. It's understanding that you're building a successful partnership, and you'll have to give in on some of these things. That's a skill. It's an art. You can't find what points to give in on and which facts to hold on to in a treatise or on a bookshelf; it's very fact- and circumstance-specific, and the issues and solutions change from deal to deal.

At all points, you want to preserve a way out. In doing so, you want to avoid things like "nevers," "non-negotiables," and "must haves." And you always want to be able to give a hook for the other side to hang their hat on, a way of saving face. After you fully understand and persuasively communicate the business issues that are driving the other side and those that are driving your side and then propose a solution, you want to make sure you provide a graceful exit to allow the other side to save face and get on to the next point. This is particularly useful if the businessperson on the other side finds your rationale or justification compelling, and you now need to bring his or her lawyer around.

One situation I try to avoid is where one businessperson talks to a lawyer, and the other businessperson talks to a lawyer, and the two lawyers speak. Unless it's a very good deal-maker lawyer who understands the issues, the last thing you want to do is engage in a discussion when people don't have the authority to concede or compromise on a point. All that does is add a three-hour conversation so they can transcribe comments and give them to their client. The more that's at stake, the bigger the deal, the more critical it is that everyone gets together in the same room, or at least in the same phone conversation. You want to make sure the businesspeople can hear the rationale behind every point. Most of the points you end up sticking on are very important to both companies, and everyone needs to understand the motivations driving these decisions. Very often in direct interaction, after you have framed the issues, the businesspeople are able to arrive at a compromise much more quickly than if the bid-and-ask is translated back and forth between two lawyers.

In my view, the difference between good deal makers and great deal makers is that great deal makers, while they get the optimal deal for their client, also figure out how to make both sides walk away from the table thinking they got their cake and ate it too. There are some very good deal makers who are more slash-and-burn types. They come in and really beat you up, and they can get a good result for their client. It's not the wrong way to approach things, but an even better result is getting a good deal for yourself as well as the other side, which can often yield tangible and intangible dividends well into the future. Ultimately, whether or not it is a good deal, there is so much goodwill generated from the deal-making and relationship-building process that it sends the businesspeople off on a very good note. The deals from which I exit shaking my head in appreciation are the ones where the other side has left happy, too. There are some large deal-doing companies that have this nailed, that have good business development teams and lawyers who work with them who understand how to go in and motivate the seller of a business and make the management team feel wonderful about it. They also understand how to negotiate the deal well. Being good at it is making sure you get what your client needs, but also understanding what the other side needs to make things go smoothly.

Caution: Dozens of Moving Parts

It's important to identify the various constituencies within a client's organization and make sure they are properly prepared for what to expect. Management may actually be multiple constituencies. For example, the CEO, the CFO, sales, and engineering may all have separate stakes and points of view. Another group to consider is the board of directors, and there can be multiple constituencies there as well. Venture-backed clients or venture-capital investors have one way of looking at things, and a corporate investor on the board, for example, may have a different set of motivations he or she brings to the table. You must also consider the client's other professional advisors, such as investment bankers and accountants, who may play significant roles in the transaction.

We spend time getting our clients to tell us what is driving them in the particular transaction in order to better understand how active various constituencies may be in the deal. For example, if it's a merger, the board is certainly going to be active, and an independent committee may be set up. We will need to sit down with the members and find out their perspective and what is driving the basis for the deal in their minds. The dynamic of who is truly sitting at the table can vary greatly, depending on, for example, whether it's a technology licensing deal or a large acquisition or the sale of the company. Each of these constituencies needs to understand the process and what to expect. Having a basic understanding and comfort level with the process helps them to buy in to the result.

You also can't neglect basic preparation. There's always a document at hand – a term sheet you're negotiating or a merger agreement or a financing document – that you must be fully familiar with, as well as with the prior deals that either party has done, particularly if they are public. You don't want to make a statement and then have the other side pull up a deal your client has already done that contradicts your position. Although there are certain ways to try to deal with the other side calling you on something (such as saying that the client's corporate policy has changed since the time of the cited prior deal), it's better to avoid the situation altogether.

An important strategy while negotiations are in progress is to have key team players remain focused on identifying and developing alternatives to the deal at hand. Viable alternatives, which may simply be a clear willingness to go it alone, not only add to your leverage in negotiations, but the possibility of following another path can also serve as a catalyst for generating a sense of urgency in the other side and moving the current deal forward more rapidly. Even if, in reality, viable alternatives are long shots or at very early stages, it is helpful to create the impression that the deal being negotiated is not your only alternative. Keep in mind that the lawyers, the investment bankers, or the judicious use of a board member can be helpful in this process.

When negotiating, it is important to listen to what the other side has to say. In my view, it's important that everybody understands the business or legal needs behind each comment. Try not to use non-negotiables, because deals develop and evolve, and the decision makers you represent, whether or not they're at the table, can often come back and compromise on a point you may have pitched as being non-negotiable. If they want to negotiate, it undermines your credibility.

It is important to know when it's time to settle or give in on your position. Part of this is realizing the importance of listening and being aware of what is happening at the table. You learn a great deal from the negotiating tactics of the other side. Some negotiators are very straightforward and constantly look for compromises to help get a deal done. If they search out compromises nine out of nine times, and on the tenth point they say that this point is established corporate policy and they can't negotiate it, you could look through prior examples of deals they have done and realize that they have never given in on this point. If I've done my homework and pulled down the prior deals to the extent that they are publicly available, I can have an associate quickly look through and vouch that that is indeed the case.

Situations can escalate at times, and if, for example, the CEO on the other side of the table seems fairly set in his or her ways, you can take a break and discuss that dynamic with your client. You have to take the temperature of the other side at different times throughout the process and constantly suggest alternatives or compromises. That's when it's important to have command of the issues and a broad base of experience behind you, so you can constantly approach issues from different angles and suggest compromises or alternatives. If you continue to run up against the same point, and the other side is able to articulate a valid business or legal reason they need to stick on that point, then perhaps it is time to leave that behind and go forward. Again, you have to talk to your own client and understand whether it is something they can ultimately live with.

There are different methodologies for managing a deal, depending on whether it's a merger, a venture-capital financing round, or a technology licensing agreement. It is important to make sure your support team is in place, not only across levels of seniority, but also across disciplines. You cannot underestimate the importance of specialists who know how their particular expertise fits into the overall deal, and who also understand that their advice needs to be tempered by practical suggestions and business savvy tailored to the specific circumstances at hand. This approach enables the team to better provide comprehensive, integrated legal and business solutions.

Doing a deal involves not just the negotiations, but also a lot of planning and execution with a myriad of details. For example, in almost every deal heavy due diligence is needed to investigate whether, among other things, there are other material agreements that affect the transaction in important ways. It's critical to make sure you line up the team and that you have both businesspeople and legal people who can do the due diligence and review the appropriate agreements. There are many, many moving pieces at this level as well, involving not just the negotiations but also bringing in tax or intellectual property or litigation people or other experts who act as consultants and strategic advisors, and it is important to make sure that everyone is on the same page. When you have three dozen moving parts, you have to make sure all those parts are being moved down the field at the same rate, so you don't wake up, having finally struck a deal, and realize that all these other pieces need to be put in place before it can get done.

Taking Command of a Deal

It's important to identify the main points of contact on the two sides. Ideally, it's the lawyers and single business contacts, and then the goal is to constantly keep in touch with your own business contact to make sure you are on the same page regarding what is being communicated and to touch base frequently regarding tactics and strategy. To the extent that there are other areas of contact, such as investment bankers, you have to continue to coordinate updates. For example, separate tax negotiations can be conducted concurrently with the business negotiations, while the diligence process continues on a somewhat independent basis. As deal manager, you need to constantly keep in touch to make sure that everything is moving forward on a coordinated and consistent basis, and that the work is being done well and on time. A lot of people are at your command, and you have to make sure everyone is getting the job done and funneling communications through the main contact people.

The team is everything. There are so many aspects to larger deals that you need many people behind you to make sure everything gets done well and on time. Matching the level of experience appropriately to the corresponding level of need is important to make sure the deal is done correctly and at a reasonable cost. You don't want to plan for people at a high billing rate to be doing diligence, and if you plan properly, you will be able to get the right level of expertise applied at the right level. Having a team of smart people who are well trained and have a good attitude means you can respond quickly and turn on a dime. You can negotiate multibillion-dollar deals in days, if need be, and make sure every issue is put to bed in the proper order.

This process doesn't just happen when you get the initial phone call from the client regarding a deal; this process is an inextricable part of the whole fabric of the business of providing legal services. It starts from day one and requires constant training and education, constantly giving attorneys direct experience in a multitude of deal situations beginning at a very early stage in their development. It's important to have represented a wide range of business enterprises in your early years of development. You have to build that experience slowly. The base for doing an exceptional job on a deal is set months and years ahead of time.

The management of risk comes in at a variety of levels. The most urgent risk is that of getting the deal done or losing it. That overarching risk is always there. It's important to understand at a very early stage the needs of the client and the alternatives available to the client if the deal does not get done. Whether or not the client has viable alternatives goes a long way in determining whether or not the team has leverage. Whether you should compromise or concede has a lot to do with how important the deal is for your client and how many alternatives you may have. On that level, it's important to constantly keep in touch with the constituencies you've identified and for your client to understand what their appetite is to continue to negotiate or whether there are other alternatives available.

While doing any deal, the prime risk is the passage of time. You never know what's going to happen tomorrow, whether it's something with your client, the business of the other side, a competitor, or the economy as a whole. There's a constant risk of an unforeseen event happening that could derail negotiations. In any transaction we face, there is always pressure to do it as fast as possible to minimize the risk of the unexpected. For example, any of our clients could in theory be subject to a lawsuit or a claim that their intellectual property infringes on that of another company. One of those letters can come out of the blue any day of the year. You can never know what tomorrow might bring, so there is always pressure to get the deal done as fast as possible.

So much of preparation relates to rapidly identifying and bringing to bear the appropriate resources so you can provide the highest quality of legal services on a timely basis. It's important to be able to turn on a dime, to provide expertise across a range of competencies and disciplines (such as business advice, tax advice, intellectual property analysis and litigation risk analysis), and to be able to bring that expertise to the table right away, deal with the issues, and keep the process moving.

Advice From the Trenches

You could have the best-written contract or merger agreement or legal document, but if you don't have an effective remedy, the agreement may not be worth much. One of the things I constantly think about – and tell my associates to think about – is, what is the remedy? And is it an effective remedy? Every legal document is a binding agreement. The whole reason you're doing a deal is to get the other side to agree to do something – to affect a merger or a distribution arrangement or to hand over a lot of money. Every deal has immediate and ongoing obligations for both parties. The question is, what is the remedy if the other side intentionally breaches or simply is unable to perform for reasons entirely outside their control? And by remedies, I don't mean only lawsuit claims. Very often litigation is not an effective remedy for the issue at hand because of the timing or the cost, or because the client actually wants to affect conduct, not necessarily receive damages. Effective remedies may include simply getting a seat at the negotiating table or making the situation unfavorable for a third-party interloper.

Another piece of advice is to continually take a step back and listen to what your client or the other side is trying to get at. Think outside the box. Think of different approaches, and suggest alternative ways of looking at or tackling a problem. Often you can find common ground by approaching a problem in a slightly different way.

As I said before, a key piece of deal advice is to fully understand what your client wants out of the deal. Don't get caught up in a lot of provisions or the wrong deal point. Make sure you explain to the client, if necessary, how the specific provisions of the agreement affect the overall objectives. For example, in a venture-capital investment, many of the entrepreneurs and management people are very concerned about ownership percentage, without realizing that they may be ceding control of the enterprise through other contractual techniques, such as restrictive covenants or voting agreements that make their ownership percentage irrelevant in an analysis of control. You must remind the client that without capital, their idea will never become a reality, or worse, someone else may beat them to the punch. It's much more important to get the capital and get the deal done in some realm of acceptability, and not hang on to issues that are of less importance. Understand that you will have to give in on some points, but at the end of the day, what is most important is to get the deal done. If you're successful in this, then your client is empowered to do what they set out to do: manufacture a product, employ people, build a business, and carry on their dream. To do so, there are certain things on which you and they will have to compromise.

Nothing beats experience, so you always have to keep yourself on the front line. You can't be an armchair quarterback. If you turn yourself into an advisor or consultant, so you are available only to answer questions, that's fine, but you keep your edge by actually being in the deal. I continue to do deals because I enjoy being an active player in the trenches. Another thing you have to keep up on is general developments in the industry – not just legal changes, but business changes, too. Keeping track of other deals and legal developments is continuing education and is an essential part of the job. Finally, you look for ways to share the experience with other top practitioners. That can be outside of the firm through bar association meetings, but we also do a lot of work internally to make sure we leverage experience across the firm. We have frequent internal seminars and discussion groups with senior associates and partners on sharing deal experience – for example, focusing on mergers and acquisitions, financings, or complex licensing deals. We have brown-bag lunches to share war stories or talk about issues and current developments. You need a combination of actively doing deals, continuing legal education, and making sure you leverage the experience from across a broad practice of not only business lawyers, but lawyers in other practice groups as well.

In my view, the golden rules of deal making include:

❑ Never lose your focus on your client's goals.
❑ A better outcome for your client is not only getting an optimal deal for the client, but also getting a deal the other side is happy with.
❑ Avoid absolutes, and always leave a way out, both for yourself and the other side.

❏ Never lose your temper unless you've planned to lose your temper.

❏ Keep the lines of communication open with your client and their other advisors.

❏ Always keep your team informed and motivated.

Patrick Ennis, ARCH Venture Partners, Partner

Preparing for a Deal

Ideally, the best preparation for a deal is to go into it with an existing personal or professional relationship with the other parties involved in the deal. Please note that I resist using the popular phrase "other side of the table" to refer to the other parties in the deal. As I repeatedly emphasize, successful early-stage venture-capital negotiations are all about building and preserving long-term positive relationships. The phrase "other side of the table" implies winners and losers and focuses the attention on the deal mechanics. For early-stage venture capital, the focus always needs to be on long-term value creation, which occurs only as a by-product of building great, unique, and innovative companies.

At our firm, we often have existing relationships with the other parties involved in the deal. For instance, all of us were formerly either entrepreneurs, businesspeople, scientists, or various combinations thereof. Most of my career, before I joined the venture-capital profession, was spent in the worlds of science, engineering, product development, and marketing. I wasn't focused solely on financial transactions or subtleties of the law; I was more focused on products and innovation. So now when I negotiate a deal in a venture-capital transaction, I have credibility and a lot in common with the entrepreneur and the others involved. To me that is a great strength, one that is much more important than being able to negotiate the last dollar in a deal.

I do early-stage venture capital, where nobody knows the exact value of the transaction. These are not later-stage companies where you can measure the cash flows down to the nearest cent. So it is really not so important that you strike the best financial terms; more important is that you strike the best terms that will allow the company to grow, and then when the company is a billion-dollar company in several years, everyone will be happy. Even if you have a perfect transaction – when you have negotiated that final cent, which is often what they teach you on Wall Street and in business school – you may have blown the relationship, which may poison the working relationship going forward.

Doing a venture deal is a lot like getting married. You need to ensure mutual trust and respect, because there is a three- to seven-year time horizon before the financial exit. The entrepreneurs we work with enjoy working with us because we had a great deal of real-world experience in science, technology, and business before we entered the venture-capital profession. Frankly, many technology entrepreneurs have a healthy disdain for cookie-cutter VCs who have never worked in a lab, developed a real product, or managed a real business. Entrepreneurs usually don't respect investment banking or consulting experience. The entrepreneurs may be polite and not let you know that, but trust me, savvy entrepreneurs can size up VCs very quickly.

When you are an early-stage venture capitalist, your personal and professional lives are heavily mixed together. Many of my close personal friends are people I work with and vice versa. There are many reasons for this. Some of it is self-selection – for example, the folks who go to Wharton for an MBA or Yale for a Ph.D. in physics tend to get involved in interesting endeavors as the years go by. Since I spent time at both of those institutions, my personal friends from those days often pop in and out of various mutual business endeavors. Also, as a venture capitalist, my value to the entrepreneurs we fund and the limited partners who entrust their money to us is maximized as we build our networks.

Much of our time at our firm is spent forging relationships with new, talented people and world-class research institutions. If you constantly add intelligent, successful people to your network, your performance as a venture capitalist is bound to improve. And time is on our side! As every year goes by, friends and colleagues tend to achieve new goals and get promoted to new positions of power and influence. It has been seventeen years since I graduated from college, and I find it amazing to read of the interesting pursuits my former classmates are involved in. And shame on me if I don't make the effort to get in touch and stay in touch, to see if I can come up with something interesting to work on together.

It is very common for venture capitalists and the founders of a company to go out on social engagements before, during, and after the deal. Often family members are invited, and the line is certainly blurred between business and personal time. We like to get to know everyone, and it is valuable to see people in different situations and realize that they are in for the long run. It makes things a little more personal.

At a high level, the correct strategy going into a deal negotiation is to know everything about the technology of the new company, the potential markets for its products, and the people who are doing the negotiation. There is no excuse for being unprepared. Among other things, being prepared shows the entrepreneurs that the negotiation is entirely in good faith and that I want to put the deal together because I have passion for their idea and want to help make it a reality. After all, venture capitalists are ultimately service providers – we are here to help entrepreneurs realize their dreams. That is the driving force behind all successful venture capitalists. It is not a passion for making money; rather, it is a passion for helping entrepreneurs build great companies. Of course, if you help build many great companies, you will generate substantial financial returns for all parties involved, especially the limited partners of the venture capital fund. And thus the cycle can begin anew.

The system works only if substantial financial returns are generated; this allows limited partners to recycle some of those returns back into new funds, which allow new cash to be disbursed to deserving entrepreneurs. But if the emphasis is on making money and not on building great companies, people will lose focus and the cycle will break. I cannot emphasize this point enough.

On the other hand, Wall Street folks are often transaction-focused. That works for them. Since they are in a different business, they have different goals, different responsibilities, different training, and different sources of capital. Early-stage venture capitalists are not transaction-focused. We are more like the entrepreneur. We get involved with the entrepreneur early on, and we want to help build a great company. Of course, good venture capitalists need to be very financially savvy and need to be experts at transactions because that is part of the job, but that usually isn't the main focus. In my ideal world, I strive to build and maintain the reputation and track record that would cause every entrepreneur, scientist, or engineer to want to work with me more than anyone else in the world.

You need to prove yourself constantly in this business, and earn the right to work side by side with the world's best entrepreneurs. At our firm, we serve on the boards of all of our investments, and that is not a responsibility we take lightly. Every day we wake up and view the day as another chance to excel. The focus is always on building great companies and doing whatever it takes to facilitate that.

At the beginning of the deal structuring and the negotiation process, it is important to be prepared and have your homework completed. Otherwise, at best, the entrepreneur may view you as just a source of money, or, at worst, he or she may decide to take money from another source because you haven't demonstrated your worth.

There are many ways to do your homework, including spending a lot of time with the entrepreneurs, understanding what they do, having many lunches and dinners, meeting their families, having them meet your family, and having them meet all of your partners. I don't try to impress them, but I let them know I understand their area, and I emphasize relevant past experiences. This way, when it comes time for the actual negotiation, its main focus is not simply to paper over the transaction with help from some attorneys, but rather to complete the transaction and get on with the business of building the company.

You should never take for granted or take lightly the dreams of entrepreneurs, because their ideas are often what they are devoting their lives to. Therefore, while the consummation of the transaction itself is a significant milestone, and should be celebrated as such, the real fun and challenge comes in executing on the business plan and building a great company. That is my deal-making strategy:

I go into it in such a way that the entrepreneur or scientist does not even feel that it's a transaction – that it's more of a milestone along the way to building a great company.

If you have been involved completely in the process leading up to the negotiations, you are already prepared for them. You should not have to stay up and "cram" the night before as if for an exam. But it is absolutely critical that before the negotiation you know how badly all parties want a deal, what the motivations are, and what the styles and personalities are. You need to know all the details about their business. You don't want to keep asking such questions as, "What are the financial projections for the third year?" You need to know the revenue projections because you have to be able to negotiate in real time. So if the entrepreneur says the valuation is too low, you need to be able to say something along the lines of, "Let's discuss this issue. Here's the way we looked at it, based on the following facts we have. Please let me know what you think..." Then a productive discussion can ensue, as opposed to your being unprepared to back up terms and conditions, in which case you will look foolish flipping through documents in real time, trying to come up with an answer. You will not be thought highly of if you cannot keep most (if not all) of the facts in your head and if you cannot be smart and think in real time. Being smart and hardworking is the price of admission to sit at the entrepreneur's side, and they deserve no less.

Likewise, when it comes down to the legal structures and the detailed term sheets, you never want to say, "I don't know about that – we'll let the lawyers worry about it." Or, "Let me call my lawyer. I'm not sure." You should know it; you should have all the facts in your head and be able to explain the minutiae. Of course, the lawyers will eventually have to review all final documents, but the point is that a venture capitalist must have a diverse skill set and be a jack-of-all-trades.

Gerard S. DiFiore, Reed Smith, Corporate & Securities Group Head

---

Understanding Client Needs

When I am approaching a deal and looking at all the moving parts, I try my best to understand my client's objective, and I ask myself: "What do they think they really need?" And then I ask: "What does my experience tell me they really need?" Those two things are often not the same, unless I am dealing with a very experienced client who has been down that particular path before. If it is an entrepreneurial client, those universes may overlap, but rarely do they correspond completely.

I try to make sure I educate the client and give them the vicarious benefit of all of my experience. In many ways – and this is why deal lawyers often end up on the business side after years and years of doing deals – many deal lawyers feel they are much better at this game than their clients, even at making business decisions. They would probably not admit to that, but it is often true. So the goal is to try to transfer the knowledge and the experience you have to the client, so the client comes away with that higher level of understanding. That is very gratifying. If the client gets that education, it creates a great bond of loyalty. Some people might say, "If you do that, you may reduce dependency because you're not the expert anymore." That's the wrong way to look at it. In my view, anyone who looks at it that way is shortsighted and is missing the boat. The best lawyers are those who empower their clients.

It is a great thing when a client comes to you and says, "Not only did you do the deal for me, and that was great, but you also educated me in the process of doing deals." That education you gave the client is something they appreciate because they view it as a bonus over and above what they expected. That also builds personal relationships, which is part of the payback to me. Getting the paycheck is great – no qualms there. But the real payback is the relationships I've built, the friendships I've created, and, probably most importantly, the knowledge that companies I have worked with have done good things and made products that benefit the world.

Succeeding in Deal Making as an Individual

Successful deal makers have four key characteristics. These are, in no particular order:

❑ You have to be a good listener. You have to listen carefully not only to what is said, but also to what is meant, and understand the real message.

❑ You have to maintain a sense of creativity and adaptability to be a good deal maker because directions often change. Things move around in a deal; nothing stands still.

❑ To be a great deal maker, you need to be able to focus at more than one level. You need to be able to focus at the macro level of the issues, and you also need to make sure the right people focus on the micro level of specifics that may also be important. The devil is in the details.

❏ The final element of successful deal making is having the energy and the persistence to create and maintain deal momentum. You have to be highly energetic, you have to be a fast study, and you have to be adaptable. You have to be able to take something you have done for somebody else and mold it into something that works for your current situation without reinventing the wheel.

Having the Guts to Walk Away

Most people do not have the guts to walk away from a deal. And most do not know how to be a gutsy negotiator in a polite, businesslike manner. You do not have to be a nasty, disgusting person to be a forthright, forceful, aggressive negotiator. And most clients do not recognize the power of being able to walk away. I think I try to instill that in clients but I'm not as successful as I would like. I say, "Don't always look at what you give up if you don't do the deal – look at what you give up if you do do the deal." It all has to do with associations and whether people look at a transaction as a way of either avoiding pain or pursuing something good.

Most humans think and act in ways that guide them to avoid pain, but few think and act in ways to pursue pleasure. Let's take that into the client context. Once people have gone down the road to do a deal, they think the other side will get angry or upset, or their synergistic relationship with them will be destroyed when they walk. They get locked into thinking that.

People have to remember that the best loss may be their first loss. It is the same thing with investors who invest in a company and then realize it was a mistake. Now what do they do? Do they put more good money after bad, or do they say, "My best loss is my first loss." The smart investors in my view take the latter approach. If you have made a mistake, it's a mistake. If you can't fix it, don't try. Have the power to walk away. I think nowadays that is a tough thing, when people have so many portfolio companies they are trying to nurse along, and investors have become so gun-shy that they do not want to pull the trigger on anything new.

But I have been involved in situations where investors – the ones I think are the smartest ones – say to themselves, "You know what? This was a mistake. Let's get over it. We're not perfect. Let's take the ego out of it and make the smart choice, which is to do nothing more." I have seen many deals consummated that were actually failures because clients didn't have the guts to walk away before the deal was done, because they had taken too much ownership in the process. They failed to realize that they had lost all perspective, and that the deal that they wanted in the beginning is not what they got at the end of the day.

These things don't fail on day one, but later. Many are catastrophic failures that tragically ruin lives. Doing a deal is like getting married. Going into it, you think the person walking down the aisle is the love of your life; but when you look across and are about to exchange vows, you pause and think, "Wait a minute! That's not the person I thought it was – it's somebody else." You are at the altar; all the witnesses are there; the families are there; and you think, "This is the wrong thing to do." It's difficult to walk away.

It's the same with deals. When you are in a deal, you have all the professionals, the businesspeople, and the bankers around you, and there is a certain level of ceremony to all of it. You still need to be able to gracefully say, "This isn't the right thing, and these are the reasons. I want to shake hands and go away friends, but we're not doing this deal."

John M. Abraham, Battery Ventures, Venture Partner

The Deal Maker

The art of deal making is akin to the act of transforming a partially molded block of clay into a work of fine art. Although many aspects of deal making, such as valuation or legal documentation, are more scientific than artistic, a good deal maker, like an artist, must have an unorthodox approach to problem solving. In an artistic sense, the deal maker envisions the finished product and molds the transaction in a way that may not have been imagined before. Deal making involves a great deal of creativity, which is why formulaic, "cookie-cutter" deals are more like signing up a franchisee than creating a partnership.

Along with creativity, the characteristics of a good deal maker include honesty, empathy, and a willingness to understand the other side's point of view. It is important to be knowledgeable about the market, and it helps to be articulate, energetic, and reasonably gregarious. A strong work ethic is essential; a good deal maker must be able to tolerate frustration and a roundabout approach to the goal.

In a pure sense, the best deal makers are those who are highly conversant with the content of what is being discussed, as opposed to those who simply steward the process. It is easy for people who aren't experienced in transactional business to make the mistake of always being in a selling mode. It is much more important to be a balanced listener and end up with a genuine understanding of what the other side is doing. You also need to understand the concepts and the level of performance a company relies upon. Command of detail makes the difference between a great and an average practitioner. In addition, the best deal makers keep their objectives in mind at all times. It's relatively easy to get carried away with the idea of getting the deal done at all costs. It's also fairly common for people in deal-making situations to get emotional and to take things personally. But it's best to remember that all deals are done for business reasons, and that achieving a reasonable outcome requires great objectivity.

Like anything else, luck and timing should never be underestimated. These factors assist great deal makers as much as anything else.

Kenneth K. Bezozo, Haynes and Boone, Partner and Section Chair, Business Transactions

Egos, Emotions, and Education

The art of good deal making is the art of understanding not only the business issues present in a transaction, but also the parties' emotions and the leverage in the transaction, and being able to layer all of these factors together with the objective of reaching a common goal – completing the transaction in a manner that works for everyone involved.

This is of particular importance in transactions that involve private (non-public) companies. Many times, in connection with this type of transaction, the attorney is dealing with only one or two people who will control the deal, and in these circumstances, the egos and personal motivations of the parties can become much more of a force to contend with than when dealing with public companies. Regardless of the nature of the transaction or the number of individuals involved, the attorney, to be an effective deal maker, must be able to develop a rapport with and an understanding of all the people who are on the various sides of the transaction.

To this end, one of the most important characteristics of being a deal maker, rather than a deal breaker, is not taking "no" for an answer, particularly when that answer is motivated by ego, emotion, or personal matters relevant to only one individual. In deal making, the attorney must realize that he will run into perceived brick walls time and again. As a result, the attorney's attitude must be that there is no brick wall he cannot go under, over, or around.

In trying to push a deal across the finish line, the attorney must, first and foremost, identify what is actually motivating his client, as well as the other party or parties to the transaction: Why has each party agreed to this transaction? At the most elementary level, the motivating factor is usually money. Occasionally, though, the attorney will discover other motivating factors, such as timing or, as already mentioned, ego. For example, sometimes one or more of the parties, perhaps more often the seller, will agree to the transaction simply because the timing is right for that party, or for reasons personal to that seller – for instance, that he wants to complete a transaction with that particular buyer. Regardless of the motivating factors, having a good understanding of those particular factors helps the attorneys and the other businesspeople involved overcome the problems and issues that surface during the course of the transaction. Additionally, the attorney must be able to identify the relative strength or weakness of each person's leverage with respect to a transaction. Only with a good understanding of the factors motivating the parties to a particular transaction, and the leverage each of those parties brings to bear on that transaction, can an attorney determine the most effective and efficient means to facilitate a successful completion of the deal.

Aside from determining his or her client's motivations and leverage, one of the most significant challenges for any transactional attorney is dealing with presidents, founders, entrepreneurs, and the like, because of the personality factors that materialize when dealing with such individuals. Generally, these people are sellers who have successful companies and are often independently wealthy – a combination that frequently breeds an exaggerated ego. Usually, to bring such a person to the negotiating table, and ultimately across the finish line, the attorney must find a way to gain a measure of control with respect to that person and the accompanying ego issues.

Despite their business successes and indubitable intelligence, often these types of sellers have rarely been involved in this kind of transaction and have no comprehension of the legal ramifications of a transaction. Such a seller may, for example, have no concept of what a representation or a warranty is, or that following the closing he may be called upon to indemnify the other party for a breach of a representation, warranty, or covenant contained in the transaction documents. All he knows is that he is going to receive millions of dollars for his business, and he wants that money in his pocket as soon as possible. The attorney will have to be particularly diligent in educating this kind of seller, and explaining, for instance, that he might have to return a part of the purchase price if there is an indemnification claim. It is imperative that the attorney discuss these issues and the mechanics of the transaction with the client from the very beginning of the process.

The client must realize that no matter how simple the transaction, there will be some difficulties that the client and the attorney will have to work through and some issues to which reasoned and educated decision-making must be applied before the transaction is actually closed. If the attorney has prepared the client with respect to these issues up front, then the process will certainly be much smoother.

When to Walk Away

Unfortunately, despite his or her best efforts and a client's motivation to complete the transaction, the attorney will sometimes determine that what it will take to actually strike the deal is just not going to work or does not make economic sense. The attorney will occasionally encounter a situation where the two parties just completely disagree. For example, they disagree on the actual value of what they are buying and selling. At that point, there is very little the attorney can actually do. Unless the attorney can convince one party that he is either asking too much or paying too little or convince the parties to use an earnout to bridge the gap, it will be difficult to bring the parties together. In situations such as these, the best counsel the attorney can offer his client may be to cut his or her losses and terminate the transaction.

It is, of course, never the attorney's decision to walk away from a deal; this decision always remains with the client. In this regard, the attorney should always advise the client of any reservations he or she may have regarding the client's benefit in proceeding with the transaction. For example, in representing a buyer of a business, if the attorney becomes concerned about the credibility or honesty of the seller (or his counsel), it is imperative that the attorney advise the client about the situation. Similarly, in representing a seller in a transaction in which the consideration is something other than cash, it is incumbent upon the attorney to inform the seller of potential creditworthiness issues. If the attorney has concerns that the buyer may not be able to make the payments required under a note, and that unless the buyer obtains funding, its common stock will be worthless, the attorney should suggest to the seller that he or she insist on more cash up front and forego notes and equity as part of the consideration. If the seller is not willing to sell the business for the cash the buyer is paying at closing, the attorney must explain to the seller that there is a reasonable likelihood that the up-front cash is all the seller will ever receive. By informing the client of these concerns, the attorney has put the client in a position to determine whether to proceed with the transaction at all or whether more due diligence is necessary.

Robert Chefitz, APAX Partners, General Partner

Nuances of Negotiating

If you must step away from a deal, the deal becomes harder to realize. Usually, through negotiations, people can be brought back to their original premise. If they stay true to the essence of their business mission – that which made them attractive at the outset – then negotiating has a great chance of succeeding, despite the initial setback. If that does not occur, the discussion will struggle to move forward.

For instance, the party may be hung up on the issue of compensation. A counter-argument to this issue follows logically. For a company X size, compensation needs to be Y, according to size. If logical reasoning falls on deaf ears, then negotiation is not occurring in good faith.

If a deal progresses extremely slowly, a third party will be brought in to freshen negotiations. This third party needs to be a good counselor, not just an attorney, and one who will understand the essence of the deal and hold both parties to task. Quite simply, he will encourage concessions from both sides. If the intervention of an attorney fails, the only remaining option is to turn to another partner. Introducing a new partner brings a rejuvenating freshness to the negotiations, and a unique, sometimes unseen, perspective that can help move a deal along. The bottom line is that a negotiator must be willing to bring a fresh face into the deal.

Negotiating is like chess. Great chess players know they are playing three or four moves ahead; so, too, with great negotiators. It is too easy to negotiate one move at a time and trap your interests in a corner. The focus must be on the end game, on the principles of the big picture, and on your purpose. A chess player plays to win, and the most effective strategy in fulfilling this purpose is to be four or five moves ahead, to avoid checkmate.

Once you know negotiating and the basic terms of the current negotiation, such as the business and the vision of the other party, the negotiation becomes second nature. You need to stay mentally flexible. I do not do a lot of preparation, or thinking about where I want a negotiation to go. An initial strategy planned in advance may prove effective, but sometimes one has to react to the flow of the negotiation as a chess player must adapt to the flow of the game.

This flexibility, however, must include seeing the big picture the deal presents. Successful negotiating breaks into two parts. First, I must convince the others of the big picture of the deal. Second, I must find a convincing and fair premise on which the deal is to succeed. It is easy to get people to agree to the big picture, but agreeing to the proposed premise is a little harder. It often occurs that a deal is two-thirds of the way to completion when the company returns and says it loves the big picture, but the previously agreed upon premise suddenly seems incredibly lopsided. Then we must re-start the deal and negotiate a new premise.

Negotiating Advice

The best piece of advice I ever received regarding negotiating was that it does not really matter. It is important to put the deal in the context of the bigger picture. It is easy to get lost in a win-or-lose mentality. Just focus on the deal or the company at hand. This approach is reinforced in that in our business you often don't know whether you've won or lost for five to six years. Sometimes a successful negotiation is one closed with no great "shake." Obviously, there is a lot of hoopla around closing and winning, but if that distracts you, sloppy business plans can sometimes sneak through the process undetected. Staying focused in negotiation means asking yourself if true goal alignment between the venture business and the entrepreneur has been achieved. If the goals are askew, yet you dance the dance for the sake of dancing, it will be a bad marriage – a long, hideous, horrible marriage…and divorce is expensive.

Honing your skills as a deal maker requires mentoring; you need to be very involved in deal negotiations from the beginning. The venture business operates in a journeyman fashion. The partner overseeing your early career will want you to be in every negotiation possible. First you will be a passenger, then a copilot, then you will fly solo. This process is important because it allows you to be there as an observer first, without the pressure of the negotiation, which helps develop your negotiating skills.

When negotiating as a team, the team has to work together smoothly. You cannot have someone running off as a cowboy, negotiating something that is inconsistent with the deal as it stands. The team needs to be on the same page. If you have someone acting out of line, you either have to defend the integrity and authority of that rogue team member, or you leave them out to dry and steer the negotiations back to the desired limits. If you contradict a senior negotiator, you ruin his or her effectiveness as a negotiator with that company.

Good individual deal makers need to be personable. They need to enjoy people's company. If the entrepreneur enjoys the company of the venture investor, he will be more willing to compromise than he would with a nasty and adversarial investor. Quite simply, you have to be someone people want to do business with. When there is an abundance of capital and an abundance of smart men with capital, the entrepreneur asks himself, "Who do I want to be married to for five or six years?"

Other important factors in negotiating include the ability to communicate well and efficiently. You need to be able to find out what is important to the other side; it may not be important to you, but it may be something you are willing to trade for.

Similarly, the best thing entrepreneurs can do when negotiating with a venture capitalist is to give the appearance that although they really want to do a deal with you and are willing to execute and go forward, there are alternatives in the wings. In the absence of alternatives, negotiations can get distracted, and the situation can be taken advantage of. I think some entrepreneurs feel that the presence of another date would make them unfaithful. They reveal this attitude too quickly. They need to say, "I told you I am dating, and I will continue to date up until the point where I say, 'I do.'"

Mary Ann Jorgenson, Squire, Sanders & Dempsey, Coordinator of Business Practice Area

The Attention Factor

Deal making requires extraordinary attention, not only the focused kind (which makes certain all the issues are covered in the negotiations, and the documents and the details are accurate), but also the scattered kind of focus that comes from having all your antennae up – noticing the body language of the participants, picking up on cues that suggest there may be more to a certain comment or fact than has yet been disclosed. At the same time you have to be sure your own body language and comments are not giving away more information than you intend!

The attention factor also plays a large role in your perceived value to your client. His trust in you is built on prior experience – your ability to sense when he needs assurance or an explanation of what impact certain language in a contract may have two years down the road, and your ability to sense which issues he would want to decide himself (and no two clients have the same list). Making sure the client is kept as "close" to the deal process as his comfort zone requires, and, just as importantly, bring alternatives to his attention even when he has not asked you to find them – these behaviors separate the really strong deal makers from the merely competent.

Friendly vs. Hostile Deals

In a friendly deal, you'll have tense moments, and three or four potential deal-breaker issues. Different companies have different levels of tolerance, for example, for environmental problems. You have to find out how to share the pain of potential environmental liabilities in a way that satisfies both parties. So there is negotiation; there is tension; there are two sides to lots of issues. But both parties want to get to the same goal line – where one wants to sell and one wants to buy – otherwise, we wouldn't be talking.

In a contested deal, nothing is agreed, including having any conversation at all. If you're being attacked, you don't want the other person in the room. If you're the raider, you want to get enough stock in your hands so that you can control the company, whether you do it with a proxy contest or a real offer to buy shares. None of it is friendly or genteel.

When the deal is hostile, I meet with my client, and we go down every road we can think of to a satisfactory result, trying to anticipate what issues will come up. Then I move into a mode of total toughness, even though I am not always conscious of it. I insist on playing by the rules – federal and state securities and corporate laws apply to hostile offers. If the other side goes over the line, I use the rules to try to get them back in line. It's total attention, total focus, and total toughness.

When the deal is friendly, I often talk with my client about whether it's worth it to make some new piece of knowledge a big issue. For example, the seller didn't tell us there was a problem at a major manufacturing facility, but we found out about it anyway, during due diligence. Is it really worth making this a big issue, when we're going to need their cooperation on fourteen other items? We're going to need them to support us with their employees, so their employees don't leave before we buy the company. We're going to need them to cement customer relationships and help us through the transition in customer relationships. I think the wiser course is to pick your fights; don't go at the other side tooth and nail over every little issue.

In both friendly deals and unfriendly deals that involve price, I think getting the pricing right is the most challenging part for both the businesspeople and the lawyers.

Teamwork Invaluable for Success

Deal making is a very personal thing – you bring your own personality and your own way of handling people and handling issues to the table. That's part of it. The other part of it is your firm's ability to provide very high-quality support: excellent associates, excellent tax input, top-notch antitrust talent.

Now my firm is providing all of this globally. The last deal I did involved facilities in nineteen countries. We had antitrust lawyers in Brussels doing the European Union part and antitrust lawyers in Washington; they all had to work together. We had filings in Spain, the Czech Republic, Germany, Portugal – we had to have seamless teamwork, with talent and resources. You can't be a successful deal maker by yourself.

Making deals is different with regard to different specialties. On the tax side, where my firm has extraordinary talent, someone often says, "You can't do it this way." They know my next request will be to find a way to do what the client needs. Eventually, they get there. They find a way to do what we want to do. They bring a value that, in a way, can't be compensated.

On the antitrust side, when you get right down to the core, the talent lies in being able to define the markets in which the companies are operating broadly enough so that if these two companies combine, they don't have a big percentage of the particular market. You don't have an antitrust problem if you have a lot of competitors left after the proposed transaction. If Company A's purchase of Company C means they'll have forty percent of the market, you're starting up a very long hill. If the market is seen as big enough that when you combine the two, they have only ten percent, that's a winner. You need the kind of talent that can think creatively about markets – keep talking to the businesspeople to learn enough about the products to be able to spark some creativity in the businesspeople, to spark another definition, another viewpoint, another vision of what the market is – and also be able to convince the regulators that their definition is correct. Often, businesspeople are paid to show they have a huge share of the market for their products. We're asking them to think bigger, differently, so the market is something else, where the combined business will have only a small share. This is quite a challenge, and the people who do it well are very, very valuable.

Invaluable Advice

One of my partners once said to me, "Mary Ann, there are at least fifteen ways to say, 'Screw you.' You don't have to be totally direct all the time." I've tried to take that to heart because I'm a very direct person.

When I'm giving advice to our youngest people, the second- and third-year associates, I find myself saying, "You need to be aware of some of the politics here." There are politics in every deal – intra-buyer and intra-seller politics. A lot of decoding of even what your client is saying depends on the context – the political context, or sometimes it's merely the business context: Has the business been doing well? Who has access to what information? Don't just go blithely around asking the client's people questions. You don't even know who knows about this deal. You have to be very careful where you step.

When I'm working with older associates – sixth- or seventh-year associates – they are really handling the diligence, the documents, and a lot of the details. They'll come to me when they want advice about how to resolve an issue, or how to get beyond this particular failure. We talk about it, and I give them what I think is just totally common-sense advice. Or I'll call the client and get through the barrier because that's what I'm there for. But so much of the advice I give is common sense and practical thinking it through. The golden rules of deal making apply here: Get prepared. Be practical. Stay contained and calm.

You Can't Be a Wimp

To become a leader in making deals, lawyers have to show either senior partners in the law firm who have worked with them or a client who will use them again that they are calm, that they have practical solutions, that they are team players, that they don't fight with people just for the sake of fighting, that they are intent on making something happen, and that they have the respect of others in their firm and others in the business.

Obviously, you can't be a wimp and be a deal maker. If somebody smells that you can't manage the deal, it just won't work. You have to look like, act like, and be a manager of process, of information, of people. I think it comes pretty naturally with experience.

There are many variations of deal management. If the deal starts with one CEO talking to another CEO, and they really think this is a good combination, and they know the price range and other conditions, then one of them comes to me and we'll talk: How much time do you think we have to get this done? What's reasonable? What are the next steps? Often the CEO says he'd like to get together a week from now and talk about the major issues. This process takes on a life of its own; it has its own schedule. I "staff" it. I get people in the firm who will be on the team, and we start looking at what we need to do in terms of diligence. We get the facts about whether we're buying or selling stock or assets and which subsidiaries hold these assets. We have a number of checklists for diligence, and we figure out the one that fits this situation and start there. You just start going, right away.

Deal Making After September 11

Before September 11, 2001, I would have said that consolidation is a process that is undeniable. You can't argue against it, except when it reduces competition to the point where the markets and regulators can't stand it. But consolidation and globalization go hand in hand, and the issue that is beginning to pop up is companies in other countries asking themselves how much of their investment they really want in the U.S. because we are going to be under siege for quite some time. That will change business.

Now, I still think we're on a path of simultaneous globalization and consolidation. I think American businesspeople are becoming much more culturally sensitive; they know they have to have locals running the businesses they own in other countries. They know they're not always going to have a common language. And they're adjusting to that.

The face of the world is going to be very, very diverse; the face of business is going to be very, very diverse – and increasingly so. So how does that affect deal making?

This increasing diversity makes deal making both far more complex and far more challenging because it's harder to identify the issues that really matter. There are issues that are hard because of language, and some cultural differences that don't really matter and some that do, and it's hard to tell the difference, as we're just getting into this period. I think it's going to be extremely interesting and challenging to make the right decisions, to take the right risks, to trust the right people.

The Format of Aspatore Law Review

Aspatore Law Review is an interactive journal based on the submission of white papers, articles and knowledge excerpts from Chair/partner level lawyers from the world's top firms.

Each Aspatore Law Review follows the following special format, specifically designed by leading lawyers as the preferred way to comprehend business intelligence:

I. Executive Summary
The Executive Summary provides the highlight of the current journal, and enables you to very quickly scan the most important concepts.

II. ALR Feature
The ALR Feature focuses on a current topic affecting all lawyers, from a variety of different Chair Level perspectives.

III. In the Know
In the Know features knowledge excerpts from leading lawyers on a variety of topics, enabling lawyers to expand their breadth of knowledge, communicate intelligently on a wide range of important issues, and develop ideas for innovation and new revenue opportunities (for themselves and their clients) within their own area of expertise.

IV. The Hot Spot
The Hot Spot section highlights a particular industry or topic that is on the brink of undergoing significant changes that will result in a multitude of legal issues that need to be addressed that will affect the majority of businesses/individuals in some way or another and provides opportunities for growth and new profit centers.

V. Profession Spotlight
The Profession Spotlight focuses on the profession of being a successful lawyer (on a personal and professional basis) and the future of a wide range of legal issues that will affect all lawyers over the next 5 to 10 years.

VI. Ideas for Innovation
Ideas for Innovation features brief one-line ideas for innovation from leading lawyers featured throughout the issue. The section also features a series of questions that can be used as a starting point for an executive meeting, brainstorming session, or distributed to key lawyers as a way to stimulate new ideas.

The Format of Aspatore Technology Review

Aspatore Technology Review is an interactive journal based on the submission of white papers, articles and knowledge excerpts from CTO level professionals from the world's top companies.

Each Aspatore Technology Review follows the following special format, specifically designed by technology professionals as the preferred way to comprehend business intelligence:

I. Executive Summary
The Executive Summary provides the highlight of the current journal, and enables you to very quickly scan the most important concepts.

II. ATR Feature
The ATR Feature focuses on a current topic affecting executives in every industry, from a variety of different C-Level (CEO, CFO, CTO, CFO, CMO, COO, Partner) perspectives.

III. In the Know
In the Know features knowledge excerpts from leading professionals on a variety of topics, enabling executives to expand their breadth of knowledge, communicate intelligently on a wide range of important issues, and develop ideas for innovation and new revenue opportunities within their own area of expertise.

IV. Industry Spotlight
The Industry Spotlight section highlights a current industry, or part of an industry, where a new type of technology is affecting the majority of businesses in some way or another and providing opportunities for growth and new profit centers.

V. Profession Spotlight
The Profession Spotlight focuses on a key C-Level (CEO, CFO, CTO, CFO, CMO, COO, Partner) or executive position, and the "Golden Rules" of that profession and other topics that will enable other types of executives to identify efficiencies, new product/service ideas, new revenue opportunities, interact better and implement innovative concepts into their own profession.

VI. Ideas for Innovation
Ideas for Innovation features brief one-line ideas for innovation from leading executives featured throughout the issue. The section also features a series of questions that can be used as a starting point for an executive meeting, brainstorming session, or distributed to key managers as a way to stimulate new ideas.

**To Order, Visit Us At www.Aspatore.com Or
Call Toll Free 1-866-Aspatore (277-2867)**

The Format of Aspatore Entrepreneurial Review

Aspatore Entrepreneurial Review is an interactive journal based on the submission of white papers, articles and knowledge excerpts from partner level venture capitalists and C-Level (CEO, CTO, CFO, CMO) executives from the world's top firms and companies.

Each Aspatore Entrepreneurial Review follows the following special format, specifically designed by venture capitalists and entrepreneurs as the preferred way to comprehend business intelligence:

I. Executive Summary
The Executive Summary provides the highlight of the current journal, and enables you to very quickly scan the most important concepts.

II. AER Feature
The AER Feature focuses on a specific topic currently affecting venture professionals and entrepreneurs.

III. In The Know
In the Know features knowledge excerpts from leading venture professionals and entrepreneurs on a variety of topics, enabling you to expand your breadth of knowledge, communicate intelligently on a wide range of important issues, and develop ideas for innovation and new revenue opportunities within your own area of expertise.

IV. Executive Perspectives
Executive Perspectives feature white papers on a variety of topics affecting venture professionals and entrepreneurs, submitted by partners from leading venture firms.

V. Profession Spotlight
The Profession Spotlight focuses on a key C-Level (CEO, CFO, CTO, CFO, CMO, COO, Partner) or executive position, and the "Golden Rules" of that profession and other topics that will enable other types of executives to identify efficiencies, new product/service ideas, new revenue opportunities, interact better and implement innovative concepts into their own profession.

VI. Industry Spotlight
The Industry Spotlight section highlights current industries (such as wireless, technology, health care, services and more), or part of an industry, that is affecting the majority of businesses in some way or another and provides opportunities for growth and new profit centers.

VII. Ideas For Innovation
Ideas for Innovation features a series of question blocks that can be used as a starting point for an executive meeting, brainstorming session, or distributed to key partners or management team executives as a way to stimulate new ideas.

**To Order, Visit Us At www.Aspatore.com Or
Call Toll Free 1-866-Aspatore (277-2867)**

The Format of Aspatore Marketing Review

Aspatore Marketing Review is an interactive journal based on the submission of white papers, articles and knowledge excerpts from C-Level (CEO, CTO, CFO, CMO) executives from the world's top companies and advertising and public relations firms.

Each Aspatore Marketing Review follows the following special format, specifically designed by marketing, advertising and public relations professionals as the preferred way to comprehend business intelligence:

I. Executive Summary
The Executive Summary provides the highlight of the current journal, and enables you to very quickly scan the most important concepts.

II. AMR Feature
The AMR Feature focuses on a current topic affecting every type of marketer, from a variety of different C-Level (CEO, CFO, CTO, CFO, CMO, COO, Partner) perspectives.

III. In the Know
In the Know features knowledge excerpts from leading professionals on a variety of marketing, advertising and public relations topics, enabling executives to expand their breadth of knowledge, communicate intelligently on a wide range of important issues, and develop ideas for innovation and new revenue opportunities within their own area of expertise.

IV. Industry Spotlight
The Industry Spotlight section highlights a current industry, or part of an industry, that is affecting the majority of businesses in some way or another and provides opportunities for growth and new profit centers.

V. Profession Spotlight
The Profession Spotlight focuses on a key C-Level (CEO, CFO, CTO, CFO, CMO, COO, Partner) or executive position, and the "Golden Rules" of that profession and other topics that will enable other types of executives to identify efficiencies, new product/service ideas, new revenue opportunities, interact better and implement innovative concepts into their own profession.

VI. Ideas for Innovation
Ideas for Innovation features brief one-line ideas for innovation from leading executives featured throughout the issue. The section also features a series of questions that can be used as a starting point for an executive meeting, brainstorming session, or distributed to key managers as a way to stimulate new ideas.

To Order, Visit Us At www.Aspatore.com Or
Call Toll Free 1-866-Aspatore (277-2867)

The Format of Aspatore Investing Review

Aspatore Investing Review is an interactive journal based on the submission of briefings, articles and knowledge excerpts from partner level investment advisors and C-Level (CEO, CTO, CFO, CMO) executives from the world's top investment firms and companies.

Each Aspatore Investing Review follows the following special format, specifically designed by investors as the preferred way to comprehend business intelligence:

I. Executive Summary
The Executive Summary provides the highlight of the current journal, and enables you to very quickly scan the most important concepts.

II. AIR Feature
The AER Feature focuses on a specific topic currently affecting all investors.

III. In The Know
In the Know features knowledge excerpts from leading investment professionals on a variety of topics, enabling you to expand your breadth of investment opportunities, communicate intelligently on a wide range of important issues, and develop ideas for innovation and new revenue opportunities.

VI. Risk Spotlight
The Industry Spotlight section highlights current industries (such as wireless, technology, health care, services and more), or part of an industry, that is affecting the majority of businesses in some way or another and provides opportunities for growth and new profit centers.

V. Tax Spotlight
The Tax Spotlight section, written by leading CPAs, focuses on both existing and new tax laws that affect investors.

VI. Alternative Investments
The Alternative Investments section focuses on additional investment opportunities such as real estate investing, private equity investing and other investment vehicles that can and should be utilized by all investors to balance an investment portfolio and provide new areas for growth.

VII. Executive Perspectives
Executive Perspectives feature white papers on a variety of growth and profitability topics affecting investors submitted by partners from leading investment firms.

VIII. The Hot Spot
The Hot Spot section highlights a particular industry or niche within an industry that is on the brink of undergoing significant changes that will result in a multitude of investment opportunities and/or risks to existing shareholders.

**To Order, Visit Us At www.Aspatore.com Or
Call Toll Free 1-866-Aspatore (277-2867)**

The Format of Aspatore Business Review

Aspatore Business Review is an interactive journal based on the submission of white papers, articles and knowledge excerpts from C-Level (CEO, CTO, CFO, CMO, Partner) executives from the world's top companies.

Each Aspatore Business Review follows the following special format, specifically designed by executives as the preferred way to comprehend business intelligence:

I. Executive Summary
The Executive Summary provides the highlight of the current journal, and enables you to very quickly scan the most important concepts.

II. ABR Feature
The ABR Feature focuses on a current topic affecting executives in every industry, from a variety of different C-Level (CEO, CFO, CTO, CFO, CMO, COO, Partner) perspectives.

III. In the Know
In the Know features knowledge excerpts from leading professionals on a variety of topics, enabling executives to expand their breadth of knowledge, communicate intelligently on a wide range of important issues, and develop ideas for innovation and new revenue opportunities within their own area of expertise.

IV. Industry Spotlight
The Industry Spotlight section highlights a current industry, or part of an industry, that is affecting the majority of businesses in some way or another and provides opportunities for growth and new profit centers.

V. Profession Spotlight
The Profession Spotlight focuses on a key C-Level (CEO, CFO, CTO, CFO, CMO, COO, Partner) or executive position, and the "Golden Rules" of that profession and other topics that will enable other types of executives to identify efficiencies, new product/service ideas, new revenue opportunities, interact better and implement innovative concepts into their own profession.

VI. Ideas for Innovation
Ideas for Innovation features brief one-line ideas for innovation from leading executives featured throughout the issue. The section also features a series of questions that can be used as a starting point for an executive meeting, brainstorming session, or distributed to key managers as a way to stimulate new ideas.

VII. What it Means
What it Means is a one-page summary by the editor of ABR, discussing the conclusions of the current journal and areas to watch going forward.

To Order, Visit Us At www.Aspatore.com Or
Call Toll Free 1-866-Aspatore (277-2867)

ASPATORE BUSINESS REVIEWS-ORDER FORM

Call Us Toll Free at 1-866-Aspatore (277-2867)
Or Tear Out This Page and Mail or Fax To:
Aspatore Books, PO Box 883, Bedford, MA 01730
Or Fax To (617) 249-1970 (Preferred)

Name:

E-mail:

Shipping Address:

City: State: Zip:

Billing Address:

City: State: Zip:

Phone:

Please Circle the Journal (s) You Would like to Subscribe to:
Aspatore Business Review   Aspatore Entrepreneurial Review
Aspatore Marketing Review   Aspatore Technology Review
Aspatore Law Review   Aspatore Investing Review

Lock in at the Current Rates Today-Rates Increase Every Year
Please Check the Desired Length Subscription:
1 Year ($1,090) _____   2 Years (Save 10%-$1,962) _____
5 Years (Save 20%-$4,360) _____   10 Years (Save 30%-$7,630) _____
Lifetime Subscription ($24,980) _____

Number of Subscriptions _____ (3-4 subscriptions-10% discount, 5-10 subscriptions-15% discount, 11-20 subscriptions-20% discount, 21-50 subscriptions-30% discount, 51+ subscriptions-40% discount) If multiple year subscription is ordered, discount will be added to previous discount. If nothing is entered, we shall process the order for 1 subscription.

(If mailing in a check you can skip this section but please read fine print below and sign below)
Credit Card Type (Visa & Mastercard & Amex):

Credit Card Number:

Expiration Date:

Signature:

Would you like us to automatically bill your credit card at the end of your subscription so there is no discontinuity in service? (You can still cancel your subscription at any point before the renewal date.) Please circle: Yes   No

*(Please note the billing address much match the address on file with your credit card company exactly)

Terms & Conditions-We shall send a confirmation receipt to your e-mail address. If ordering from Massachusetts, please add 5% sales tax on the order (not including shipping and handling). If ordering from outside of the US, an additional $51.95 per year will be charged for shipping and handling costs. All issues are paperback and will be shipped as soon as they become available. Sorry, no returns, cancellations or refunds at any point unless automatic billing is selected, at which point you may cancel at any time before your subscription is renewed (no funds shall be returned however for the period currently subscribed to). Issues that are not already published will be shipped upon publication date. Publication dates are subject to delay-please allow 1-2 weeks for delivery of first issue. If a new issue is not coming out for another month, the issue from the previous quarter will be sent for the first issue.

**To Order, Visit Us At www.Aspatore.com Or
Call Toll Free 1-866-Aspatore (277-2867)**

BUILD YOUR OWN BUSINESS LIBRARY

Option A: Receive Every Book Published by Aspatore Books-Only $1,089 a Year- A Savings of Over 60% Off Retail prices

Receive every book published by Aspatore Books every year-between 60-100 books-a must have on bookshelves of every executive and an invaluable resource for quick access, business intelligence from industry insiders. Or send the collection as a gift to someone else!

The Aspatore Business Library Collection features must have business books on various positions, industries and topics, creating the ultimate business library for business professionals. The books in the collection feature business intelligence from C-Level executives (CEO, CTO, CFO, CMO, CFO, Partner) from the world's most respected companies, and represent an invaluable resource for quick access, business intelligence from industry insiders on a wide range of topics. Every business professional should have their own executive library, such as the top executives and great business leaders of our time have always had. The Aspatore Business Library Collection features the most exclusive, biggest name executives of our time and their most insightful words of wisdom, creating the ultimate executive library. Upon order being placed, you will immediately receive books published within the last month, and then for 11 months going forward (you also receive all titles 1-3 months before retail stores receive the new book). You may even request up to 10 books already published by Aspatore Books to be included.

Option B: 25 Best Selling Business Books-Only $399-A Savings of Over 45%Off Retail Prices!

Buy the top 25 best selling business titles published by Aspatore Books, a must have on bookshelves of every executive and an invaluable resource for quick access, business intelligence from industry insiders. Or send the collection as a gift to someone else! These books feature business intelligence from C-Level executives (CEO, CTO, CFO, CMO, CFO, Partner) from over half the world's 500 largest companies. Although every book may not be in your exact area of specialty, having these books on hand will time and again serve as incredible resources for you and everyone in your office. These books provide a wide array of information on various positions, industries and topics, creating a complete business library unto themselves. If you already have one or more of these books, please note this on the order form and different books will be added.

To Order, Visit Us At www.Aspatore.com Or Call Toll Free 1-866-Aspatore (277-2867)

Books Included:

Inside the Minds: The Wireless Industry-Industry Leaders Share Their Knowledge on the Future of the Wireless Revolution

Inside the Minds: Leading Consultants-Industry Leaders Share Their Knowledge on the Future of the Consulting Profession and Industry

Inside the Minds: Leading Deal Makers-Industry Leaders Share Their Knowledge on Negotiations, Leveraging Your Position and the Art of Deal Making

Inside the Minds: The Semiconductor Industry-Industry Leaders Share Their Knowledge on the Future of the Semiconductor Revolution

Inside the Minds: Leading Advertisers-Industry Leaders Share Their Knowledge on the Future of Advertising, Marketing and Building Successful Brands

Inside the Minds: Leading Accountants-Industry Leaders Share Their Knowledge on the Future of the Accounting Industry & Profession

Inside the Minds: The New Health Care Industry-Industry Leaders Share Their Knowledge on the Future of the Technology Charged Health Care Industry

Inside the Minds: Leading IP Lawyers-Leading IP Lawyers Share Their Knowledge on the Art & Science of Intellectual Property

Inside the Minds: Leading Labor Lawyers-Leading Labor Lawyers Share Their Knowledge on the Art & Science of Labor Law

Inside the Minds: Leading Litigators-Leading Litigators Share Their Knowledge on the Art & Science of Litigation

Inside the Minds: The Art of Public Relations-PR Visionaries Reveal the Secrets to Getting Noticed, Making a Name for Your Company, and Building a Brand Through Public Relations

Inside the Minds: Venture Capitalists-Inside the High Stakes and Fast Moving World of Venture Capital

Bigwig Briefs: Term Sheets & Valuations-An Inside Look at the Intricacies of Term Sheets & Valuations

Bigwig Briefs: Hunting Venture Capital-An Inside Look at the Basics of Venture Capital

Inside the Minds: Leading Wall St. Investors-Financial Gurus Reveal the Secrets to Picking a Winning Portfolio

Inside the Minds: Leading Marketers-Industry Leaders Share Their Knowledge on Building Successful Brands

Inside the Minds: Chief Technology Officers-Industry Experts Reveal the Secrets to Developing, Implementing, and Capitalizing on the Best Technologies in the World

Inside the Minds: Internet Bizdev-Industry Experts Reveal the Secrets to Inking Deals in the Internet Industry

Inside the Minds: Entrepreneurial Momentum-Jump Starting a New Business Venture or Taking Your Business to the Next Level

Inside the Minds: Internet Bigwigs-Internet CEOs and Research Analysts Forecast the Future of the Internet Economy

Inside the Minds: Leading CEOs-The Secrets to Management, Leadership & Profiting in Any Economy

Inside the Minds: Internet Marketing-Industry Experts Reveal the Secrets to Marketing, Advertising, and Building a Successful Brand on the Internet

Inside the Minds: Leading CTOs-Industry Leaders Share Their Knowledge on Harnessing and Developing the Best Technologies

Bigwig Briefs: Guerrilla Marketing-The Best of Guerrilla Marketing

Oh Behave! Reinforcing Successful Behaviors at Work With Consequences

**To Order, Visit Us At <u>www.Aspatore.com</u> Or
Call Toll Free 1-866-Aspatore (277-2867)**

BUILD YOUR OWN BUSINESS LIBRARY

Call Us Toll Free at 1-866-Aspatore (277-2867)
Or Tear Out This Page and Mail or Fax To:
Aspatore Books, PO Box 883, Bedford, MA 01730
Or Fax To (617) 249-1970 (Preferred)

Name:

E-mail:

Shipping Address:

City: State: Zip:

Billing Address:

City: State: Zip:

Phone:

Please Check Option A or Option B:

Option A _____ (Receive Every Book Published by Aspatore Books-$1,089 a Year)
Please indicate here any titles already published by Aspatore Books you would like in addition (there will be no charge for these titles as they will be included as part of the first month of books):

_____

_____

_____

_____

Option B _____ (25 Best Selling Business Books-$399)
Please indicate here any titles you already currently have (other best selling titles on a similar topic will then be added in their place):

_____

_____

(If mailing in a check you can skip this section but please read fine print below and sign below)
Credit Card Type (Visa & Mastercard & Amex):

Credit Card Number:

Expiration Date:

Signature:

If option A is chosen, would you like us to automatically bill your credit card at the end of your subscription so there is no discontinuity in service? (You can still cancel your subscription at any point before the renewal date.) Please check: Yes _____   No _____

*(Please note the billing address much match the address on file with your credit card company exactly)

Terms & Conditions-We shall send a confirmation receipt to your e-mail address. If ordering from Massachusetts, please add 5% sales tax on the order (not including shipping and handling). If ordering from outside of the US, an additional $300 in shipping and handling costs will be charged for Option A and an additional $125 for Option B. All books are paperback and will be shipped as soon as they become available. Total number of books for Option A will vary from year to year, between 60-100 books. Sorry, no returns or refunds at any point unless automatic billing is selected, at which point you may cancel at any time before your subscription is renewed (no funds shall be returned however for the period currently subscribed to). Books that are not already published will be shipped upon publication date. Publication dates are subject to delay-please allow 1-2 weeks for delivery of first books. For the most up to date information on publication dates and availability please visit www.Aspatore.com.

To Order, Visit Us At www.Aspatore.com Or
Call Toll Free 1-866-Aspatore (277-2867)

THE FOCUSBOOK™
ASSEMBLE YOUR OWN
BUSINESS BOOK™

Ever wish you could assemble your own business book, and even add your own thoughts in the book? Here is your chance to become the managing editor or your own book!

The Focusbook™ enables you to become the managing editor of your own book, by selecting individual chapters from the best selling business books published by Aspatore Books to assemble your own business book. A Focusbook™ can highlight a particular topic, industry, or area of expertise for yourself, your team, your course, or even your entire company. You can even add additional text of your own to the book, such as reference information, points to focus on, or even a course syllabus, in order to further customize it to better suit your needs. The Focusbook™ is the future of business books, allowing you to become the managing editor of your own business book, based on what you deem important, enabling yourself, and others to focus, innovate and outperform.

How It Works:

1. Select up to 10, 15, or 25 chapters from the choices on the following pages by checking the appropriate boxes. (Each Chapter Ranges From 15-40 Pages)
2. Decide if you want to include any of your own text to the book—maybe an introduction (as to why you chose these chapters), employee instructions (for new hires or to use as a management course/refresher), a course syllabus, information so it is applicable for clients/customers (reference), or even an article/white paper you already wrote. (Please note Aspatore Books will not edit the work, it is simply printed as is. Aspatore Books will not be considered the publisher of any additions and you will retain all rights to that content.)
3. Decide on a quantity.

**To Order, Visit Us At www.Aspatore.com Or
Call Toll Free 1-866-Aspatore (277-2867)**

How the Book Will Look:
1. The book will be 5 inches tall and 8 inches wide (on the front and back). The width will vary depending on the amount of text. The book will look like a normal business book found in bookstores nationwide.

2. On the cover of the book, it will read "A Focusbook™ Assembled By," with your name on the next line (Jason Phillips in the example above). We can also add a company/university/course name if you so choose. Your name will also appear on the spine of the book. You can then also select a title for your Focusbook™ (such as Marketing Smarts as depicted in the picture above). On the back of the book will be the chapter names from your book.
3. The book will feature the standard Focusbook™ cover (see above), with the dominant colors being black with a red stripe across.
4. The chapters will be placed in a random order, unless a specific order is instructed on the order form. If you are adding your own text, it can be placed at the beginning or the end of the text.
5. The book will feature the chapters you selected, plus any content of your own (optional), and a special section at the end for notes and ideas of your own to add as you read through and refer back to your Focusbook™.

**Select the Chapters You Want on the Following Pages Then
Fill Out the Order Form at the End**

**To Order, Visit Us At <u>www.Aspatore.com</u> Or
Call Toll Free 1-866-Aspatore (277-2867)**

Chapter #/Title	Author	Units
VENTURE CAPITAL/ENTREPRENEURSHIP		
123. *Developing the Right Team Strategy	Sam Colella (Versant Ventures, Managing Director)	1
124. *Successful Deal Doing	Patrick Ennis (ARCH Venture Partners, Partner)	1
125. *Deal Making: The Interpersonal Aspects	John M. Abraham (Battery Ventures, Venture Partner)	1
126. *The Art of Negotiations	Robert Chefitz (APAX Partners, General Partner)	1
127. Future Opportunities	Michael Moritz (Sequoia Capital)	1
128. *What VCs Look For	Heidi Roizen (SOFTBANK Venture Capital)	1
129. International Opportunities	Jan Henric Buettner (Bertelsmann Ventures)	1
130. The Importance of Technology	Alex Wilmerding (Boston Capital Ventures)	1
131. Next Generation Success	Andrew Filipowski (divine interVentures)	1
132. Internet Business Models	Suzanne King (New Enterprise Associates)	1
133. Valuations and Key Indicators	Jonathan Goldstein (TA Associates)	1
134. Early Stage Investing	Virginia Bonker (Blue Rock Capital)	1
135. Calculating Risk	Guy Bradley (CMGI @ Ventures)	1
136. *Focus on Technology	Stephan Andriole (Safeguard Scientifics, Inc.)	1
137. Evaluating Business Models	Marc Benson (Mid-Atlantic Venture Funds)	1
138. Early Stage Valuations and Keys to Success	Roger Novak, Jack Biddle (Novak Biddle Venture Partners)	1
139. The Importance of People and the Market	Nuri Wissa (Kestrel Venture Management)	1
140. Focused Investing	Mark Lotke (Internet Capital Group)	1

* **Denotes Best Selling Chapter**

Chapter #/Title	Author	Units
141. *Term Sheet Basics	Alex Wilmerding (Boston Capital Ventures)	1
142. *How to Examine a Term Sheet	Alex Wilmerding (Boston Capital Ventures)	1
143. *A Section-by-Section View of a Term Sheet	Alex Wilmerding (Boston Capital Ventures)	4
144. *Valuations and the Term Sheet	Alex Wilmerding (Boston Capital Ventures)	1
145. Marketing Your Business to Investors	Harrison Smith (Krooth & Altman, Partner)	1
146. Essential Elements in Executive Summaries	Harrison Smith (Krooth & Altman, Partner)	1
267. *The Journey to Entrepreneurship	Dave Cone (Camstar, CEO)	1
268. *Founding a Business on Principles	Steve Demos (White Wave, Founder & President)	1
269. *Entrepreneur 101-From Validation to Viability	Mike Turner (Waveset Technologies, CEO)	1
270. Entrepreneurship Through Choppy Waters	Frederick Beer (Auragen Communications, CEO)	1
271. The World of Entrepreneurial Momentum	Hatch Graham (Bandwidth9, CEO)	1
271. The Extreme Entrepreneur	Todd Parent (Extreme Pizza, CEO)	1
272. *An Entrepreneur's Blueprint for Success	Farsheed Ferdowsi (Paymaxx, CEO)	1
273. From Mom & Pop to National Player	Jack Lavin (Arrow Financial Services, CEO)	1
274. Better to Be a PT Boat Than a Battleship	Lucinda Duncalfe Holt (Destiny, CEO)	1
275. *Lessons Learned for Entrepreneurs	Art Feierman (Presenting Solutions, CEO)	1
MARKETING/ADVERTISING/PR		
1. *Connecting With Consumer Needs	Stephen Jones (Coca-Cola, Chief Marketing Officer)	1
2. Staying Customer Focused	T. Michael Glenn (FedEx, EVP Market Development)	1
3. Building an Internet Mega-Brand	Karen Edwards (Yahoo!, VP, Brand Marketing)	1

* Denotes Best Selling Chapter

Chapter #/Title	Author	Units
4. Giving the Consumer a Seat at the Table	Michael Linton (Best Buy, SVP Marketing)	1
5. Building a Powerful Marketing Engine	Jody Bilney (Verizon, SVP Brand Management)	1
6. *Brands and Marketing: Evolving Together	John Hayes (American Express, EVP Brand Management)	1
7. Marlboro Friday: Branding a Product	Richard Rivers (Unilever, SVP)	1
8. Marketing Success: Providing Choice	Richard Costello (GE, Corporate Marketing Manager)	1
9. Turning a Brand Into a National Pastime	Tim Brosnan (Major League Baseball, EVP Business)	1
10. Advertisers' Conundrum–Change or Be Changed	M T Rainey (Young & Rubicam, Co-CEO)	1
11. *Rallying the Troops in Advertising	Eric Rosenkranz (Grey, CEO Asia Pacific)	1
12. Achieving Success as an Advertising Team	David Bell (Interpublic Group, Vice Chairman)	1
13. *Advertising: Invitation Only, No Regrets	Bob Brennan (Leo Burnett Worldwide, President)	1
14. *The Secret to Global Lovemark Brands	Tim Love (Saatchi & Saatchi, Managing Partner)	1
15. Soak it All In-The Secrets to Advertising Success	Paul Simons (Ogilvy Mather UK, CEO)	1
16. Likeable Advertising: Creative That Works	Alan Kalter (Doner, CEO)	1
17. Advertising Success: Tuning Into the Consumer	Alan Schultz (Valassis, CEO)	1
18. The Client Perspective in Advertising	Brendan Ryan (FCB Worldwide, CEO)	1
19. *Advertising Results in the Age of the Internet	David Kenny (Digitas, CEO)	1
20. *Communications for Tomorrow's Leaders	Christopher Komisarjevsky (Burson-Marsteller,CEO)	2
21. The Creation of Trust	Rich Jernstedt (Golin/Harris International, CEO)	1
22. *Prosumer: A New Breed of Proactive Consumer	Don Middleberg (Middleberg Euro RSCG, CEO)	1
23. *The Power of PR in a Complex World	Richard Edelman (Edelman PR, CEO)	1
24. Success in Public Relations	Lou Rena Hammond (Lou Hammond & Assoc., President)	1

* Denotes Best Selling Chapter

Chapter #/Title	Author	Units
25. The Art and Science of Public Relations	Anthony Russo, Ph.D. (Noonan Russo Communications, CEO)	1
26. Critical Elements of Success in PR	Thomas Amberg (Cushman Amberg Communications, CEO)	1
27. Small Business PR Bang!	Robyn M. Sachs (RMR & Associates, CEO)	1
28. PR: A Key Driver of Brand Marketing	Patrice Tanaka (Patrice Tanaka & Company, Inc., CEO)	1
29. PR: Essential Function in a Democratic Society	David Finn (Ruder Finn Group, Chairman)	1
30. *21st Century Public Relations	Larry Weber (Weber Shandwick Worldwide, Founder)	1
31. *Public Relations as an Art and a Craft	Ron Watt (Watt/Fleishman-Hillard Inc., CEO)	1
32. Connecting the Client With Their Public	David Copithorne (Porter Novelli International, CEO)	1
33. PR: Becoming the Preferred Strategic Tool	Aedhmar Hynes (Text 100, CEO)	1
34. Public Relations Today and Tomorrow	Herbert L. Corbin (KCSA PR, Managing Partner)	1
35. Delivering a High Quality, Measurable Service	David Paine (PainePR, President)	1
36. *The Impact of High-Technology PR	Steve Schwartz (Schwartz Comm., President)	1
37. The Emotional Quotient of the Target Audience	Lee Duffey (Duffey Communications, President)	1
38. The Service Element in Successful PR	Andrea Carney (Brodeur Worldwide, CEO)	1
39. Helping Clients Achieve Their True PE Ratio	Scott Chaikin (Dix & Eaton, Chairman and CEO)	1
40. The Art of Public Relations	Dan Klores (Dan Klores Communications, President)	1
41. Passion and Precision in Communication	Raymond L. Kotcher (Ketchum, CEO)	1
42. Professionalism and Success in Public Relations	Victor Kamber (The Kamber Group, CEO)	1
43. A Balanced Internet Marketing Program	Meg Brossy (24/7 Media, Chief Marketing Officer)	1
44. *Internet Guerrilla Marketing on a Budget	Jay Levinson (Best-Selling Author)	1
45. Narrowcasting Through Email Marketing	Joe Payne (Microstrategy, Chief Marketing Officer)	1

* Denotes Best Selling Chapter

Chapter #/Title	Author	Units
46. Targeted Internet Marketing Strategies	John Ferber (Advertising.com, Founder)	1
47. Incentive Marketing on the Internet	Steve Parker (MyPoints, SVP Marketing)	1
48. B2B Internet Marketing	Tara Knowles (Viant, Chief Marketing Officer)	1
49. Breaking Through the Clutter on the Internet	Wenda Harris (Doubleclick, EVP General Network)	1
50. Measuring ROI Across Different Mediums	Mark Delvecchio (eWanted.com, VP Marketing)	1
51. *What is Guerrilla Marketing?	Jay Levinson (Best-Selling Author)	1
52. *What Makes a Guerrilla?	Jay Levinson (Best-Selling Author)	1
53. *Guerrilla Marketing: Attacking the Market	Jay Levinson (Best-Selling Author)	1
86. *Everyone is a Marketer	Jay Levinson (Best-Selling Author)	1
87. *Media Choices for the Guerrilla Marketer	Jay Levinson (Best-Selling Author)	1
88. *Technology and the Guerrilla Marketer	Jay Levinson (Best-Selling Author)	1
107. *Guerrilla Marketing on a Budget	Jay Levinson (Best-Selling Author)	1

MANAGEMENT/ CONSULTING

Chapter #/Title	Author	Units
276. *Maintaining Values in a Culture of Change	Richard Priory (Duke Energy, CEO)	1
69. *Fundamentals Never Go Out of Style	Fred Poses (American Standard, CEO)	1
70. High-Tech Company, High-Touch Values	John W. Loose (Corning, CEO)	1
71. Balancing Priorities for the Bottom Line	Bruce Nelson (Office Depot, Chairman)	1
72. *Keeping the Right People With Your Company	Thomas C. Sullivan (RPM, CEO)	1
73. *Gaining Entrepreneurial Momentum	Myron P. Shevell (New England Motor Freight, CEO)	1

* Denotes Best Selling Chapter

Chapter #/Title	Author	Units
74. Creating a Culture That Ensures Success	Justin Jaschke (Verio, CEO)	1
54. *The Drive for Business Results	Frank Roney (IBM, General Manager)	1
55. *Understanding the Client	Randolph C. Blazer (KPMG Consulting, Inc., CEO)	1
56. *The Interface of Technology and Business	Pamela McNamara (Arthur D. Little, Inc., CEO)	1
57. *Elements of the Strategy Consulting Business	Dr. Chuck Lucier (Booz-Allan & Hamilton, SVP)	1
58. *Consulting: Figuring Out How to Do it Right	Dietmarr Osterman (A.T. Kearney, CEO)	1
195. Client Value in Consulting	Luther J. Nussbaum (First Consulting Group, CEO)	1
196. The Rules Have Changed in Consulting	John C. McAuliffe (General Physics Corporation, President)	1
197. Tailoring Solutions to Meet Client Needs	Thomas J. Silveri (Drake Beam Morin, CEO)	1
198. *The Future of Marketing Consulting	Davis Frigstad (Frost & Sullivan, Chairman)	1
59. *Setting and Achieving Goals (For Women)	Jennifer Openshaw (Women's Financial Network)	1
60. The Path to Success (For Women)	Tiffany Bass Bukow (MsMoney, Founder and CEO)	2
61. Becoming a Leader (For Women)	Patricia Dunn (Barclays Global Investors, CEO)	1
62. Career Transitions (For Women)	Vivian Banta (Prudential Financial, CEO)	1
63. Making the Most of Your Time (For Women)	Kerri Lee Sinclair (AgentArts, Managing Director)	1
64. Follow Your Dreams (For Women)	Kim Fischer (AudioBasket, Co-Founder and CEO)	1
65. Keep Learning (For Women)	Krishna Subramanian (Kovair, CEO)	1
66. Keep Perspective (For Women)	Mona Lisa Wallace (RealEco.com, CEO)	1
67. Experiment With Different Things (For Women)	Emily Hofstetter (SiliconSalley.com, CEO)	1
68. Do What You Enjoy (For Women)	Lisa Henderson (LevelEdge, Founder and CEO)	1

* Denotes Best Selling Chapter

Chapter #	Title	Author	Units
		LAW	
75.	*Navigating Labor Law	Charles Birenbaum (Thelan Reid & Priest, Labor Chair)	1
76.	The Makings of a Great Labor Lawyer	Gary Klotz (Butzel Long, Labor Chair)	1
77.	The Complexity of Labor Law	Michael Reynvaan (Perkins Coie, Labor Chair)	1
78.	*Labor Lawyer Code: Integrity and Honesty	Max Brittain, Jr. (Schiff Hardin & Waite, Labor Chair)	1
89.	The Litigator: Advocate and Counselor	Rob Johnson (Sonnenschein Nath, Litigation Chair)	1
90.	*The Key to Success in Litigation: Empathy	John Strauch (Jones, Day, Reavis & Pogue, Litigation Chair)	1
91.	*Major Corporate and Commercial Litigation	Jeffrey Barist (Milbank, Tweed, Hadley, Litigation Chair)	1
92.	Keys to Success as a Litigator	Martin Flumenbaum (Paul, Weiss, Rifkind, Litigation Chair)	1
93.	*Deciding When to Go to Trial	Martin Lueck (Robins, Kaplan, Miller, Litigation Chair)	1
94.	Credibility and Persuasiveness in Litigation	Michael Feldberg (Schulte Roth & Zabel, Litigation Chair)	1
95.	*Litigation Challenges in the 21st Century	Thomas Kilbane (Squire, Sanders, Dempsey, Litigation Chair)	1
96.	*Keeping it Simple	Evan R. Chesler (Cravath, Swaine & Moore, Litigation Chair)	1
97.	Assessing Risk Through Preparation & Honesty	Harvey Kurzweil (Dewey Ballantine, Litigation Chair)	1
98.	The Essence of Success: Solving the Problem	James W. Quinn (Weil, Gotshal & Manges, Litigation Chair)	1
99.	The Performance Aspect of Litigation	Charles E. Koob (Simpson Thacher Bartlett, Litigation Chair)	1
100.	*The Future of IP: Intellectual Asset Mngmnt.	Richard S. Florsheim (Foley & Lardner, IP Chair)	1
101.	The Balancing of Art & Science in IP Law	Victor M. Wigman (Blank Rome, IP Chair)	1
102.	*Policing a Trademark	Paula J. Krasny (Baker & McKenzie, IP Chair)	1
103.	Credibility & Candor: Must Have Skills	Brandon Baum (Cooley Godward, IP Litigation Chair)	1
104.	The Art & Science of Patent Law	Stuart Lubitz (Hogan & Hartson, Partner)	1

* **Denotes Best Selling Chapter**

Chapter #/Title	Author	Units
105. Successful IP Litigation	Cecilia Gonzalez (Howrey Simon Arnold & White, IP Chair)	1
106. Achieving Recognized Value in Ideas	Dean Russell (Kilpatrick Stockton, IP Chair)	1
108. Keeping Current W/ Rapidly Changing Times	Bruce Keller (Debevoise & Plimpton, IP Litigation Chair)	1
109. *Maximizing the Value of an IP Portfolio	Roger Maxwell (Jenkins & Gilchrist, IP Chair)	2
110. *The Power of Experience in Deal Making	Joseph Hoffman (Arter & Hadden, Corporate/Securities Chair)	1
111. *The Deal: The Beginning Rather than the End	Mark Macenka (Testa, Hurwitz & Thibeault, Business Chair)	1
112. Communicating With Clients	Gerard S. DiFiore (Reed Smith, Corporate/Securities Chair)	1
113. Making a Deal Work	Kenneth S. Bezozo, (Haynes and Boone, Business Chair)	1
114. Challenges for Internet & Tech. Companies	Carl Cohen (Buchanan Ingersoll, Technology Chair)	1
115. The Copyright Revolution	Mark Fischer (Palmer & Dodge, Internet/E-Commerce Chair)	1
116. Privacy Rights and Ownership of Content	Brian Vandenberg (uBid.com, General Counsel)	1
117. Business Intelligence From Day One	Mark I. Gruhin (Schmeltzer, Aptaker and Shepard, , Partner)	1
118. Legal Rules for Internet Companies	Arnold Levine (Proskauer Rose LLP, Chair, iPractice Group)	1
119. Protecting Your Assets	Gordon Caplan (Mintz Levin PC)	1
120. The Golden Rules of Raising Capital	James Hutchinson (Hogan & Hartson LLP)	1
121. Identifying the Right Legal Challenges	John Igeo (Encore Development, General Counsel)	1
122. The Importance of Patents	Richard Turner (Sughrue, Mion,, Senior Counsel)	1
79. *Common Values in Employment Law	Columbus Gangemi, Jr. (Winston & Strawn, Labor Chair)	1
80. Building Long Term Relationships with Clients	Fred Alvarez (Wilson Sonsini, Labor Chair)	1
81. *Becoming Part of the Client's Success	Brian Gold (Sidley Austin Brown & Wood, Labor Chair)	1
82. *Understanding Multiple Audiences	Raymond Wheeler (Morrison & Foerster, Labor Chair)	1

* Denotes Best Selling Chapter

Chapter #/Title	Author	Units
83. Employment Lawyer: Advisor and Advocate	Judith Langevin (Gray, Plant, Mooty & Bennett, Labor Chair)	1
84. *Bringing Added Value to the Deal Practice	Mary Ann Jorgenson (Squires Sanders Dempsey,Labor Chair)	1
85. Traditional Legal Matters on the Internet	Harrison Smith (Krooth & Altman LLP, Partner)	1

TECHNOLOGY/INTERNET

Chapter #/Title	Author	Units
167. *Closing the Technology Gap	Dr. Carl S. Ledbetter (Novell, CTO)	1
168. *Creating and Enriching Business Value	Richard Schroth (Perot Systems, CTO)	1
169. *Innovation Drives Business Success	Kirill Tatarinov (BMC Software, Senior Vice President, CTO)	1
170. *Managing the Technology Knowledge	Dr. Scott Dietzen (BEA E-Commerce Server Division, CTO)	1
171. The CTO as an Agent of Change	Doug Cavit (McAfee.com, CTO)	1
172. The Class Struggle and The CTO	Dan Woods (Capital Thinking, CTO)	1
173. A CTO's Perspective on the Role of a CTO	Mike Toma (eLabor, CTO)	1
174. Technology Solutions to Business Needs	Michael S. Dunn (Encoda Systems, CTO, EVP)	1
175. Bridging Business and Technology	Mike Ragunas (StaplesDirect.com, CTO)	1
176. *The Art of Being a CTO - Fostering Change	Rick Bergquist (PeopleSoft, CTO)	1
178. Developing Best of Breed Technologies	Dr. David Whelan (Boeing, Space and Communications, CTO)	1
179. *Technology as a Strategic Weapon	Kevin Vasconi (Covisint, CTO)	1
180. Role of the CTO in a Venture-Backed Startup	Dan Burgin (Finali, CTO)	1
181. *Leading Technology During Turbulent Times	Frank Campagnoni (GE Global eXchange Services, CTO)	1
182. Staying on Top of Changing Technologies	Andrew Wolfe (SONICblue (formerly S3), CTO)	1

* Denotes Best Selling Chapter

Chapter #/Title	Author	Units
183. Building What the Market Needs	Neil Webber (Vignette, Former CTO, Co-Founder)	1
184. *Let the Business Dictate the Technology	Dwight Gibbs (The Motley Fool, Chief Techie Geek)	1
185. Technology Solutions: From the Ground Up	Peter Stern (Datek, CTO)	1
186. The Securities Behind Technology	Warwick Ford (VeriSign, CTO)	1
187. Building Leading Technology	Ron Moritz (Symantec, CTO)	1
188. The Business Sense Behind Technology	Dermot McCormack (Flooz.com, CTO and Co-Founder)	1
189. A Simple and Scaleable Technology Interface	Pavan Nigam (WebMD, Former CTO/Co-Fndr, Healtheon)	1
190. Designing the Right Technology Solution	Michael Wolfe (Kana Communications, VP, Engineering)	1
191. The Role of a CTO	Daniel Jaye (Engage, CTO and Co-Founder)	1
147. *Wireless Technology: Make It Simple	John Zeglis (AT&T Wireless, CEO)	1
148. *Bringing Value to the Consumer	Patrick McVeigh (OmniSky, Chairman and CEO)	1
149. Wireless Challenges	Sanjoy Malik (Air2Web, Founder, President and CEO)	1
150. The High Costs of Wireless	Paul Sethy (AirPrime, Founder & Chairman)	1
151. Developing Areas of Wireless	Reza Ahy (Aperto Networks, President & CEO)	1
152. *The Real Potential for Wireless	Martin Cooper (Arraycomm, Chairman & CEO)	1
153. Bringing Wireless into the Mainstream	Robert Gemmell (Digital Wireless, CEO)	1
154. VoiceXML	Alex Laats (Informio, CEO and Co-Founder)	1
155. Reaching the Epitome of Productivity	Rod Hoo (LGC Wireless, President and CEO)	1
156. Identifying Revenue Opportunities	Scott Bradner (Harvard Univ., Senior Technical Consultant)	1
157. The Wireless Satellite Space	Tom Moore (WildBlue, President and CEO)	1

* Denotes Best Selling Chapter

Chapter #/Title	Author	Units
158. *Memory Solutions for Semiconductor Industry	Steven R. Appleton (Micron Technology, Inc., CEO)	1
159. *Programmable Logic: The Digital Revolution	Wim Roelandts (Xilinx, Inc., CEO)	1
160. The Streaming Media Future	Jack Guedj, Ph.D. (Tvia, Inc., President)	1
161. Building a Winning Semiconductor Company	Igor Khandros, Ph.D. (FormFactor, Inc., President and CEO)	1
162. The Next Generation Silicon Lifestyle	Rajeev Madhavan (Magma, Chairman, CEO and President)	1
163. Semiconductors: The Promise of the Future	Steve Hanson (ON Semiconductor, President and CEO)	1
164. Dynamics of the Semiconductor Data Center	Eyal Waldman (Mellanox Technologies, LTD, CEO)	1
165. The Market-Driven Semiconductor Industry	Bob Lynch (Nitronex, President and CEO)	1
166. Semiconductors: Meeting Performance Demand	Satish Gupta (Cradle Technologies, President and CEO)	1
192. Balanced Internet Marketing Programs	Meg Brossy (Chief Marketing Officer, 24/7 Media)	1
193. Internet Ad Campaigns, Not Just Cool Ads	Brooke Correll (Wineshopper.com, VP Marketing)	1
194. Internet Advertising: Moving the Profit Needle	John Herr (Buy.com, Sr. VP Marketing & Advertising)	1
202. Future Internet Opportunities	Joe Krauss (Excite@Home, Founder)	1
203. Internet Future: An International Perspective	Charles Cohen (Beenz.com, CEO)	1
204. Valuing Internet Companies	John Segrich (CIBC, Internet Research Analyst)	1
205. The Potential for Personal Computing	Larry Cotter (Sandbox.com, CEO)	1
206. Using Innovation to Fulfill Customer Needs	Kyle Shannon (AGENCY.COM, Co-Founder)	1
207. Being a Leader in the Internet Economy	Jeff Sheahan (Egghead, CEO)	1
208. *Being a Sustainable Internet Business	Jonathan Nelson (Organic, Inc., CEO and Co-Founder)	1
209. Business-to-Business Effects on the Internet	Chris Vroom (Credit Suisse First Boston, Internet Analyst)	1

* Denotes Best Selling Chapter

Chapter #/Title	Author	Units
210. Risk & Uncertainty: Internet Co. Challenges	Joseph Howell (Emusic.com, Chief Financial Officer)	1
211. Focus on Profits in the Internet Economy	Lynn Atchison (Hoovers.com, Chief Financial Officer)	1
212. Cash Flow for Internet Companies	Tim Bixby (LivePerson, Chief Financial Officer)	1
213. Financial Accountability for Internet Companies	Greg Adams (Edgar Online, Chief Financial Officer)	1
214. Establishing Value for Internet Companies	Louis Kanganis (Nerve.com, Chief Financial Officer)	1
215. Managing Rapid Growth	David R. Henkel (Agillion.com, Chief Financial Officer)	1
216. Scalability and Profits for Internet Companies	Alan Breitman (Register.com, Chief Financial Officer)	1
217. *Building Real Value for Internet Companies	Joan Platt (CBS MarketWatch, Chief Financial Officer)	1
218. Financial Forecasting for the Internet Economy	David Gow (Ashford.com, Chief Financial Officer)	1
219. *Organizing the Internet Financial House	Mary Dridi (webMethods, Chief Financial Officer)	1
220. *Internet BizDev: Leveraging Your Value	John Somorjai (Keen.com, VP, Business Development)	1
221. Internet BizDev: Staying Focused	Todd Love (yesmail.com, Senior VP, Business Development)	1
222. Internet BizDev: Focusing on Corporate Goals	Chris Dobbrow (Real Names, SVP, Business Development)	1
223. Finding the Right Partners for an Internet Co.	Scott Wolf (NetCreations, SVP, Business Development)	1
224. Changing Internet Market Conditions	Daniel Conde (Imandi.com, Director, Business Development)	2
225. *Maximizing Time and Efficiencies	Bernie Dietz (WebCT, VP, Business Development)	1
226. Internet BizDev: Pushing the Right Buttons	Mark Bryant (LifeMinders.com, VP, Business Development)	1
227. BizDev Leadership in the Internet Economy	Robin Phelps (DigitalOwl.com, VP Business Development)	1

FINANCIAL

244. *Merging Information Tech. & Accounting	Paul McDonald (Robert Half Int'l, Executive Director)	1

* Denotes Best Selling Chapter

Chapter #/Title	Author	Units
245. *The Accountant's Perspective	Gerald Burns (Moss Adams, Partner)	2
246. New Areas for Accountants	Dick Eisner (Richard A. Eisner & Co., Managing Partner)	1
247. *Audits & Analyzing Business Processes	Lawrence Rieger (Andersen, Global Managing Partner)	1
248. Accounting & the Entrepreneurial Market	Domenick Esposito (BDO Seidman, Vice Chairman)	1
250. E-Business Transformation	Fred Round (Ernst & Young, Director of eBusiness Tax)	1
251. Accounting: The UK/US Perspective	Colin Cook (KPMG, Head of Transaction Services - London)	1
252. The Changing Role of the Accountant	Jim McKerlie (Ran One, CEO)	1
253. The Future of Accounting	Harry Steinmetz (M.R. Weiser & Company, Partner)	1

INVESTING

Chapter #/Title	Author	Units
197. Who Wants to Become a Millionaire?	Laura Lee Wagner (American Express, Senior Advisor)	1
198. *The Gold is in Your Goals	Harry R. Tyler (Tyler Wealth Counselors, Inc., CEO)	1
199. *Timeless Tips for Building Your Nest Egg	Christopher P. Parr (Financial Advantage, Inc.)	1
200. It's What You Keep, Not Make, That Counts	Jerry Wade (Wade Financial Group, President)	1
201. Accumulating Your Million-Dollar Nest Egg	Marc Singer (Singer Xenos Wealth Management)	1
228. Time-Honored Investment Principles	Marilyn Bergen (CMC Advisors, LLC, Co-President)	1
229. *The Art & Science of Investing	Clark Blackman, II (Post Oak Capital Advisors, Managing Dir.)	1
240. Altering Investment Strategy for Retirement	Gary Mandell (The Mandell Group, President)	1
241. *Fair Value & Unfair Odds in Investing	Scott Opsal (Invista Capital Mngmt, Chief Investment Officer)	1
242. Earnings Count & Risk Hurts	Victoria Collins (Keller Group Investmnt Mngmnt, Principal)	1

* Denotes Best Selling Chapter

Chapter #/Title	Author	Units
243. *Navigating Turbulent Markets	Howard Weiss (Bank of America, Senior Vice President)	1
249. Building an All-Weather Personalized Portfolio	Sanford Axelroth & Robert Studin (First Financial Group)	1
254. Managing Your Wealth in Any Market	Gilda Borenstein (Merill Lynch, Wealth Mngmt. Advisor)	1
255. Winning Strategies for International Investing	Josephine Jiménez (Montgomery Asset Mngmnt, Principal)	1
256. The Psychology of a Successful Investor	Robert G. Morris (Lord Abbett, Dir. of Equity Investments)	1
257. *Investing for a Sustainable Future	Robert Allan Rikoon (Rikoon-Carret Investments, CEO)	1
	OTHER	
258. *E-Health: The Adjustment of Internet Tech.	Robert A. Frist, Jr. (HealthStream, CEO and Chairman)	1
259. Health Care: The Paper Trail	Jonathan S. Bush (athenahealth, CEO and Chairman)	1
260. Consumer Backlash in the Health Care Industry	Peter W. Nauert (Ceres Group, CEO and Chairman)	1
261. Forging a Path in the New Health Care Industry	Dr. Norm Payson (Oxford Health, CEO & Chairman)	1
262. The Future of Clinical Trials	Dr. Paul Bleicher (Phase Forward, Chairman)	1
263. Health Care: Linking Everyone Together	John Holton (scheduling.com, CEO)	1
264. The Future of the Health Care Industry	Robert S. Cramer, Jr. (Adam.com, CEO and Chairman)	1
265. Being a Change Agent in Health Care	Kerry Hicks (HealthGrades, CEO & Chairman)	1
266. Personalized Solutions in Health Care	Dr. Mark Leavitt (Medscape, Chairman)	1

* Denotes Best Selling Chapter

THE FOCUSBOOK™

ASSEMBLE YOUR OWN BUSINESS BOOK™

Call Us Toll Free at 1-866-Aspatore (277-2867)
Or Tear Out the Next 2 Order Form Pages & Fax or Mail BOTH Pages To:
Aspatore Books, PO Box 883, Bedford, MA 01730
Or Fax To (617) 249-1970 (Preferred)

Name:

Email:

Shipping Address:

City: State: Zip:

Billing Address:

City: State: Zip:

Phone:

Book Content-5 Questions
1. What chapters would you like added? (Please list by number and author last name-i.e. 2-Jones.) (10 Units/Chapters is Standard for 1 Book.):

_____

_____

_____

_____

_____

_____

_____

2. If you are adding content, do you want it put at the beginning or end of the book? _____
3. Would you like the chapters in a particular order? (If this part is not filled out, we shall put them in random order.) If so, please list by author in order from first to last:

_____

_____

_____

4. How would you like your name to read on the cover? (If you would like a company/university/course name added as well, please list it here with your name.): _____
5. What would you like the title of the book to be? (If none is added, we will simply put the information from the previous question.):

_____

To Order, Visit Us At www.Aspatore.com Or
Call Toll Free 1-866-Aspatore (277-2867)

Pricing-3 Steps

1. Quantity:

1 Book – $99   **2 Books** – $198 ($99 Per Book)
5 Books – $445 ($89 Per Book)**10 Books** – $790 ($79 Per Book)
50 Books – $2,450 ($49 Per Book) **100 Books** – $3,900 ($39 Per Book)
250 Books – $7,250 ($29 Per Book)   **500 Books** – $10,500 ($21 Per Book)
1000 Books – $15,000 ($15 Per Book) **5000 Books** – $49,750 ($9.95 Per Book)

Number of Books: _____ *Price for Books:* _____

2. Decide the Number of Chapters in Your Book (If you are selecting only 10 units or less, please skip to No. 3-units are based on number of pages-most chapters are 1 unit, however some are more depending on length.)

10 Units (Standard-Approximately 200-250 Pages) – No Extra Charge
15 Units – Please Add $25 Per Book if Ordering Between 1-10 Books, Add $15 Per Book if Ordering 50-250 Books, Add $7.50 Per Book if Ordering 500-5000 Books (So if ordering 50 books, the additional charge would be 50x10=$500)
25 Units – Please Add $75 Per Book if Ordering Between 1-10 Books, Add $25 Per Book if Ordering 50-250 Books, Add $10 Per Book if Ordering 500-5000 Books (So if ordering 50 books, the additional charge would be 50x25=$1,250)

Number of Units: _____ *Price for Additional Chapters:* _____

3. Adding Content (You must order at least 50 books to add content.) (If you are not adding any content, skip this section.)

Adding 1 Page – Please Add $3 Per Book if Ordering 50-250 Books, Please Add $2 Per Book if Ordering 500-5000 Books
Adding 2-9 Pages – Please Add $8 Per Book if Ordering 50-250 Books, Add $4.00 Per Book if Ordering 500-5000 Books
Adding 10-49 Pages – Please Add $18 Per Book if Ordering 50-250 Books, Add $9 Per Book if Ordering 500-5000 Books
Adding 50-99 Pages – Please Add $25 Per Book if Ordering 50-250 Books, Add $13 Per Book if Ordering 500-5000 Books
Adding 100-149 Pages – Please Add $40 Per Book if Ordering 50-250 Books, Add $20 Per Book if Ordering 500-5000 Books

(Please base page count by single spacing, 12 point font, Times New Roman font type on 8.5X11 paper.) (Only charts and graphs that are smaller than 4 inches wide and 7 inches tall can be included.)
(A staff member will email you within 1 week of the order being placed to coordinate receiving the materials electronically.)

Number of Pages Added: _____ *Price for Pages Added:* _____

To Order, Visit Us At www.Aspatore.com Or
Call Toll Free 1-866-Aspatore (277-2867)

PLEASE REPRINT THE FOLLOWING INFORMATION FROM THE PREVIOUS PAGE:

Number of Books: _____   *Price for Books:* _____
Number of Units: _____   *Price for Additional Chapters:* _____
Number of Pages Added: _____   *Price for Pages Added:* _____
   Total Price From Sections 1-3: _____

(If mailing in a check you can skip this section but please read fine print below and sign below-check must be received before a book is started-please email jennifer@aspatore.com for an alternate address if you are going to send the check via FedEx or UPS as the PO Box will not accept such shipments.)

Credit Card Type (Visa & Mastercard & Amex):

Credit Card Number:

Expiration Date:

Signature (Acceptance of Order and Terms & Conditions): _____

IF ADDING CONTENT, AFTER FAXING/MAILING THIS FORM, PLEASE EMAIL THE CONTENT AS A MICROSOFT WORD ATTACHMENT TO JENNIFER@ASPATORE.COM. THE EMAIL SHOULD INCLUDE YOUR NAME AND FOCUS BOOK NAME. YOU WILL RECEIVE AN EMAIL BACK WITHIN 24 HOURS IF THERE ARE ANY PROBLEMS/QUESTIONS FROM OUR STAFF.

*(Please note the billing address much match the address on file with your credit card company exactly)

For rush orders, guaranteed to ship within 1 week (for orders of 10 books or less) or within 2 weeks (for orders of 50 books or more) please initial here _____. An additional charge of $100 for orders of 10 or less books, $250 for orders of 11-25 books, $500 for orders of 25-100 books will be charged. If additional information is needed on rush orders, please email jennifer@aspatore.com.

If you would like your order sent via FedEx or UPS, for faster delivery, please enter your FedEx or UPS number here: _____ Please Circle One (FedEx/UPS). Delivery Type-Please Circle (Next Day, 2Day/Ground)

FOR QUESTIONS, PLEASE CONTACT ASPATORE BOOKS VIA EMAIL AT STORE@ASPATORE.COM.

Terms & Conditions - Prices include shipping and handling, unless a rush order is placed. All books are sent via media mail. We shall send a confirmation receipt to your email address. If ordering from Massachusetts, please add 5% sales tax on the order. If ordering from outside of the US, an additional $8.95 for shipping and handling costs will be charged for the first book, and $1.95 for each book thereafter. All books are paperback and will be shipped as soon as they become available. Sorry, no returns, refunds or cancellations at any point, even before the order has shipped or any additional content submitted. Aspatore Books is also not liable for any spacing errors in the book-only printing errors as determined by Aspatore Books. Any additions to the book will be formatted in relation to the rest of the text font size and type. Publication dates are subject to delay-please allow 1-4 weeks for delivery.

Please note that the rights to any content added to the Focusbook™ shall be retained by the author, and that Aspatore Books is simply printing the material in the Focusbook™, not publishing it. Aspatore Books shall not print, publish or distribute the content in any other media, or sell or distribute the content. The rights to all other material in the book shall remain the property of Aspatore Books and may not be reproduced or resold under any condition with out the express written consent of Aspatore Books. The author warrants and represents that to the best of his/her knowledge: (a) he/she has the right to print this material; (b) he/she has no contractual commitment of any kind which may prevent him/her from printing the material; (c) the contribution does not contain any unlawful, libelous or defamatory matter and does not infringe upon the rights, including copyright, of any other person or entity. The individual adding content to the Focusbook™ agrees to assume full liability for any content added to their FocusBook™, and agrees to indemnify and hold harmless Aspatore Books, its owners, officers, employees, agents, shareholders, parents, affiliates, subsidiaries, predecessors, agents, legal representatives, successors and assignees from and against any and all suits, claims, damages, liabilities, including attorneys' fees, based on or with respect to the falsity of any representation or warranty made to Aspatore Books, whether actual or claimed, or any infringement or related claims.

To Order, Visit Us At www.Aspatore.com Or
Call Toll Free 1-866-Aspatore (277-2867)

Inside the Minds: The Semiconductor Industry-Leading CEOs Share Their Knowledge on the Future of Semiconductors (ISBN: 1587620227)
Inside the Minds: Chief Technology Officers-Developing, Implementing and Capitalizing on the Best Technologies in the World (ISBN: 1587620081)
Bigwig Briefs: Become a CTO-Leading CTOs Reveal How to Get There, Stay There, and Empower Others That Work With You (ISBN: 1587620715)
Bigwig Briefs: Small Business Internet Advisor-Big Business Secrets for Small Business Success on the Internet (ISBN: 1587620189)
Inside the Minds: Internet Marketing-Advertising, Marketing and Building a Successful Brand on the Internet (ISBN: 1587620022)
Inside the Minds: Internet Bigwigs-Leading Internet CEOs and Research Analysts Forecast the Future of the Internet Economy (ISBN: 1587620103)
Inside the Minds: Internet CFOs-Information Every Individual Should Know About the Financial Side of Internet Companies (ISBN: 158762)
Inside the Minds: Internet BizDev-The Golden Rules to Inking Deals in the Internet Industry (ISBN: 1587620057)
Bigwig Briefs: The Golden Rules of the Internet Economy-The Future of the Internet Economy (Even After the Shakedown) (ISBN: 1587620138)
Inside the Minds: Internet Lawyers-Important Answers to Issues For Every Entrepreneur, Lawyer & Anyone With a Web Site (ISBN: 1587620065)

LAW
Inside the Minds: Leading Labor Lawyers-Labor Chairs Reveal the Secrets to the Art & Science of Labor Law (ISBN: 1587621614)
Inside the Minds: Leading Litigators-Litigation Chairs Revel the Secrets to the Art & Science of Litigation (ISBN: 1587621592)
Inside the Minds: Leading IP Lawyers-IP Chairs Reveal the Secrets to the Art & Science of IP Law (ISBN: 1587621606)
Inside the Minds: Leading Deal Makers-Negotiations, Leveraging Your Position and the Art of Deal Making (ISBN: 1587620588)
Inside the Minds: Internet Lawyers-Important Answers to Issues For Every Entrepreneur, Lawyer & Anyone With a Web Site (ISBN: 1587620065)

For More Information, Visit Us At www.Aspatore.com Or Call Toll Free 1-866-Aspatore (277-2867)

Bigwig Briefs: The Art of Deal Making-The Secrets to the Deal Making Process (ISBN: 1587621002)
Bigwig Briefs: Career Options for Law School Students-Leading Partners Reveal the Secrets to Choosing the Best Career Path (ISBN: 1587621010)

MARKETING/ADVERTISING/PR

Inside the Minds: Leading Marketers-Leading Chief Marketing Officers Reveal the Secrets to Building a Billion Dollar Brand (ISBN: 1587620537)
Inside the Minds: Leading Advertisers-Advertising CEOs Reveal the Tricks of the Advertising Profession (ISBN: 1587620545)
Inside the Minds: The Art of PR-Leading PR CEOs Reveal the Secrets to the Public Relations Profession (ISBN: 1587620634)
Inside the Minds: PR Visionaries-The Golden Rules of PR and Becoming a Senior Level Advisor With Your Clients (ISBN: 1587621517)
Inside the Minds: Internet Marketing-Advertising, Marketing and Building a Successful Brand on the Internet (ISBN: 1587620022)
Bigwig Briefs: Online Advertising-Successful and Profitable Online Advertising Programs (ISBN: 1587620162)
Bigwig Briefs: Guerrilla Marketing -The Best of Guerrilla Marketing-Big Marketing Ideas For a Small Budget (ISBN: 1587620677)
Bigwig Briefs: Become a VP of Marketing-How to Get There, Stay There, and Empower Others That Work With You (ISBN: 1587620707)

FINANCIAL

Inside the Minds: Leading Accountants-The Golden Rules of Accounting & the Future of the Accounting Industry and Profession (ISBN: 1587620529)
Inside the Minds: Internet CFOs-Information Every Individual Should Know About the Financial Side of Internet Companies (ISBN: 1587620057)
Inside the Minds: The Financial Services Industry-The Future of the Financial Services Industry & Professions (ISBN: 1587620626)
Inside the Minds: Leading Investment Bankers-Leading I-Bankers Reveal the Secrets to the Art & Science of Investment Banking (ISBN: 1587620618)

For More Information, Visit Us At
www.Aspatore.com Or
Call Toll Free 1-866-Aspatore (277-2867)

Bigwig Briefs: Become a CFO-Leading CFOs Reveal How to Get There, Stay There, and Empower Others That Work With You (ISBN: 1587620731)
Bigwig Briefs: Become a VP of Biz Dev-How to Get There, Stay There, and Empower Others That Work With You (ISBN: 1587620723)
Bigwig Briefs: Career Options for MBAs-I-Bankers, Consultants & CEOs Reveal the Secrets to Choosing the Best Career Path (ISBN: 1587621029)

INVESTING

Inside the Minds: Building a $1,000,000 Nest Egg -Simple, Proven Ways for Anyone to Build a $1M Nest Egg On Your Own Terms (ISBN: 1587622157)
Inside the Minds: Leading Wall St. Investors -The Best Investors of Wall Street Reveal the Secrets to Profiting in Any Economy (ISBN: 1587621142)

OTHER

Inside the Minds: The New Health Care Industry-The Future of the Technology Charged Health Care Industry (ISBN: 1587620219)
Inside the Minds: The Real Estate Industry-The Future of Real Estate and Where the Opportunities Will Lie (ISBN: 1587620642)
Inside the Minds: The Telecommunications Industry-Telecommunications Today, Tomorrow and in 2030 (ISBN: 1587620669)
Inside the Minds: The Automotive Industry-Leading CEOs Share Their Knowledge on the Future of the Automotive Industry (ISBN: 1587620650)

**For More Information, Visit Us At
www.Aspatore.com Or
Call Toll Free 1-866-Aspatore (277-2867)**

ASPATORE

Executive Business Intelligence